THE CONFIDENT COMMUNICATOR

OTHER TITLES BY DIANNE BOOHER

Nonfiction
Winning Sales Letters
Good Grief, Good Grammar
To the Letter
First Thing Monday Morning
Writing for Technical Professionals
The Complete Letterwriter's Almanac
A Handbook of Model Speeches for All Occasions
Cutting Paperwork in the Corporate Culture
The New Secretary
Send Me a Memo
Would You Put That In Writing?
Getting Along with People Who Don't Get Along
Making Friends with Yourself and Other Strangers
Rape: What Would You Do If . . . ?
Help, We're Moving!
Coping When Your Family Falls Apart
Love
The Faces of Death

Fiction
Boyfriends and Boy Friends
They're Playing Our Secret
That Book's Not in Our Library
Not Yet Free
The Last Caress

THE CONFIDENT COMMUNICATOR

Dianna Booher

VICTOR BOOKS®

A DIVISION OF SCRIPTURE PRESS PUBLICATIONS INC.
USA CANADA ENGLAND

DEDICATION

To my husband, Vernon

Unless otherwise noted, Scripture quotations are from *The Holy Bible, New King James Version.* © 1979, 1980, 1982, Thomas Nelson, Inc. Verses marked TLB are taken from *The Living Bible,* © 1971, Tyndale House Publishers, Wheaton, IL 60189. Used by permission.

Library of Congress Cataloging-in-Publication Data

Booher, Dianna Daniels.
   The confident communicator / Dianna Booher.
     p.   cm.
   ISBN 0-89693-779-8
    1. Public speaking—Religious aspects—Christianity.
I. Title.
PN4173.B66   1990
808.5'1—dc20
                                    90-40397
                                       CIP

---

1 2 3 4 5 6 7 8 9 10 Printing/Year 94 93 92 91 90

CONTENTS

ACKNOWLEDGMENTS

Thanks again to all the office staff for their exceptional *efforts—from timing and typing . . . to transparencies and airline tickets. They diligently see that my own presentations and speaking engagements come off as planned for our clients. Chris O'Shea once again made a diligent effort with the manuscript preparation.*

PREFACE

The silent majority has been silent too long—literally. Christians need to be more visible in the political arena, in our school systems, and in the business world. The Confident Communicator gives the necessary know-how for people to speak up and be heard. Communication—both writing and speaking—is the primary avenue of influencing our world for the better.
                                    —DIANNA BOOHER

Introduction

How do you feel when someone tells you how well things turned out after he or she took your advice in handling a situation?

Do you enjoy telling people what you think on a particular subject?

Are you sensitive to other people's reactions to what you say?

Do you talk with you hands?

Do you look people in the eye when you talk to them?

Do you catch yourself being animated in conversation and moving around with energy that seems to unconsciously flow from you?

Do you like to tell people what you've learned so they can benefit also?

Do you think visually?

Can you take a complicated idea or a complex piece of equipment and tell somebody about it fairly simply?

Do you wish you could help people understand things as clearly as you do?

Can you keep your cool under pressure?

Do you have a tendency to "get up on your soapbox" when talking about a good cause?

Is there a little bit of cheerleader in you?

After meetings do you tend to want someone to sum up what's been said? Or do so yourself?

Have you ever thought you'd like to be an actor or singer?

Do you have a desire to share your personal faith with friends and family?

If you answered "yes" to even half of these questions, chances are that you will make a great speaker. Either you have much of the natural skill required or you at least have the motivation necessary to learn to communicate effectively one-on-one or in front of groups.

☞ 1. So What's in It for You?

Speaking well:

- Helps you share your faith and influence others.
- Makes your ideas clearer to yourself and to others.
- Cements relationships.
- Builds your reputation as an intelligent person.
- Enhances your leadership skills.
- Wins respect, visibility, and recognition for your ideas and values.
- Promotes your career and earns financial rewards.
- Promotes your company and its products or services.

Our ability to succeed in all relationships depends far more than we realize on our ability to communicate— whether it's conference-room talk, cafeteria talk, or pillow talk. In fact, a lack of preparation and a weak education show up first in our communication skills—both speaking and writing. Therefore, learning to improve our skills in self-expression will pay off everywhere we turn.

Let's consider the business arena first. We all know that it's not necessarily the brightest or the most capable thinkers who get ahead. Often it's those who make a strong impact on people who can promote them or buy from them. Business professionals who speak well are considered more intelligent, more forceful, and more likable than their quieter counterparts.

One study shows that 88 percent of our on-the-job success is due to our attitudes and communication skills and only 12 percent to our technical expertise. No longer is speaking a nice-to-have skill for the business world—it's expected. And the higher one goes in the company, the more crucial the skill.

One of the key problems Exxon had in dealing with the 1989 oil spill in Alaska was that the CEO did not immediately make a public statement and go there to speak privately to those individuals wanting answers or at least apologies. Public speaking has become the norm for senior executives.

But even if you're not a senior executive explaining crises, you may often find yourself speaking before peers—either in your professional organizations or in support of personal causes. Many of us speak for a living daily; that is, we speak to customers and clients to sell products or services. Our speaking success is directly related to our commission check.

Outside the business world, we continue to find chances to put our skills to work on behalf of others— club fundraisers, political issues, farewells to friends leaving the community, Bible study classes.

When handling the truths of God, speaking well is not a choice; it's a command: "Always be ready to give a defense to everyone who asks you a reason for the hope that is in you, with meekness and fear" (1 Peter 3:15).

☞ 2. Why a Book on the Subject?

Visualize the last terrible presentation you heard. The speaker slouches in front of the group, peering out with the frightened, puzzled look of a man who's just been awakened from a bad dream. He fumbles with his notes, with the microphone, with the AV equipment. His slides look foreign to him. His impromptu comments are jumbled. When he finally gets into his subject, he keeps his eyes glued to the notes while the audience stares at their watches like scientists at a NASA countdown.

Definitely not a good role model for us. But then consider speakers we hear on TV. Politicians who ramble on, guilty of double-speak. Athletes, caught in the locker room after the big win, who roll out cliché after cliché. The Kiwanis Club president who's never conducted a business meeting before. None of these seem to have a purpose, any logical organization, or any concrete support for their opinions. Instead, they ramble in a monotone with no watch to remind them when it's over. Poor models surround us everywhere. We need some help.

Yet those of us who want to do better frequently receive little training in effective speaking because bosses assume we received the "basics" in the educational system—perhaps from giving those class book reports. Church leaders often make the same assumptions when they ask us to conduct a meeting, lead a Sunday School class, or present a recommendation to the deacons.

Despite their assumptions, most of us know better. We know that speaking well is not a natural ability—at least not all phases of it.

If the presidents and would-be presidents of the United States—after all their practice in public speaking on the way to the nomination—need speaking coaches, then two things are evident: (1) Speaking is not a natural skill. (2) Doing it right is important and effective for our cause.

So are we eager to gain that same practice and experience? Rarely.

☞ **3. Why Is Speaking So Frightening?**

Two national studies by R.H. Brushkin Associates research firm, published in the *Book of Lists*, pinpointed speaking before a group as the number-one fear for 41 percent of the population—ahead of snakes, heights, financial worries, loneliness, or death. In other words, many of us may be prepared to die and face eternity, but we're not equally prepared to speak!

We lack confidence. We worry about coming across with sincerity rather than arrogance. We worry that the audience will consider us believable and credible. We get frustrated that we're not exactly getting our point across and that we don't quite have our ideas and information organized. We fear antagonizing people. We fear embarrassing ourselves with stupid ideas, a weak and fumbling delivery of those ideas, and a noticeable case of hives. Above all, we fear letting anyone know how afraid we are.

If we're not careful, we'll fall into the trap of simply modeling what we see and hear in our equally unskilled peers—with no more success or influence than they.

Basically there are four stages to developing any skill:

Ignorance: You don't know that you don't know.

Awareness: You know you don't know.

Attention to: You work on knowing.

Inattention to: You know, and you know you know.

This book will take readers through this final stage. As you read, you'll first become aware of what makes great speakers effective. Then you'll learn where to focus your attention to model their success and have the same impact. Finally, with practice, you'll become so skilled that you no longer have to give attention to the mechanics of speaking and instead can focus on your message.

☞ 4. Is There Really a Right and Wrong Way?

Though published articles and books abound on communication skills, you'll find it difficult to sift the wheat from the chaff. Contradictory advice is everywhere. In reading previously published information, I ran across the following contradictions from speaking experts:

- Content is more important than delivery. Vs. Delivery is more important than content.
- Speaking is a performance. Vs. Speaking is just talking aloud before people.
- The audience likes you and wants you to do well. Vs. The audience must be won over.
- Always prepare and practice from a full written script. Vs. Never write out a full script.
- The overhead transparency is the best visual aid. Vs. The overhead transparency is the worst visual of all.
- Flip charts are outdated as a visual. Vs. Flip charts are effective, handy, and easily customized.
- Write on your visuals while you talk. Vs. Talk and then write.
- Use colored backgrounds for your transparencies to add variety. Vs. Never use colored backgrounds because they are less readable than clear backgrounds.
- Put your notes on index cards. Vs. Put your notes on a single sheet of paper so you can see all the ideas in one glance.
- Announce to your audience when you're about to conclude. Vs. Never announce to your audience when you're about to conclude.
- Dress formally to show respect for your audience. Vs. Dress informally to show openness.
- Repeat questions from the audience before answering them. Vs. Don't repeat audience questions.
- Put your key message at the beginning. Vs. Put your key message at the end of your talk.

And here you are reading another book, huh?

What about explanations on these contradictions? The needs of audiences, types of presentations, environments, and speaker capabilities and experience all dictate variety and flexibility. But the contradictions don't rule out the basics. Proven techniques for organizing and delivering your information to your audience—large or small—will greatly increase your impact.

And as a full-time speaker myself, I can share blunders to avoid as well as techniques that have worked with great effectiveness. I'll also be passing along tips from my observations of thousands of presenters among my client organizations—both their techniques and feedback about their impact with peers, bosses, and customers.

☞ 5. Learning from the Bible

The final authority and the best models, however, are found in the Bible. Jesus was the master speaker and teacher. He addressed large audiences from the synagogues, from the mountainside, from the seaside, and in the streets. He addressed small groups such as the Pharisees who liked to debate with Him, the disciples who wanted to learn from Him, and His friends such as Mary, Martha, and Lazarus who conversed with Him about their daily needs. He even spent His time one-on-one with the Samaritan woman at the well and the rich young ruler who came to Him by night.

By what techniques and personality traits did He create such an impact? He was prepared, and He spoke as one with authority and control. In fact, Matthew notes, after the Sermon on the Mount, "that the people were astonished at His [Jesus] teaching; for He taught them as one having authority and not as the scribes" (Matt. 7:28-29).

Yet He was patient with those slow to understand. He used both humor and anger to get His points across. His simple language awed even the most educated. He was available when those around Him had specific questions about His principles. Open and truthful, He applied His messages—from paying taxes to serving guests.

There was variety in His techniques: parables, object lessons, illustrations, analogies, paradoxes, silence, humor, role models, questioning, and lectures. He used a coin as an object lesson on taxes. He illustrated a servant's heart by washing His disciples' feet. He used a powerful silence before the accusers of the adulterous woman to convict them of their hypocrisy. And with the woman at the well He used superb questioning techniques to communicate His message about living water.

His disciples, too, began to astound those around them with speaking ability learned from the Master. "Now when they saw the boldness of Peter and John, and perceived that they were unlearned and untrained men, they marveled. And they realized that they had been with Jesus" (Acts 4:13).

They didn't let their lack of formal education hold them back from being effective speakers; nor did they let their lack of education become an excuse for not improving their skills. The Apostle Paul wrote, "Even though I am untrained in speech, yet I am not in knowledge" (2 Cor. 11:6).

Keep in mind that the disciples often had their trying times before audiences. They spoke to "neutral" listeners in large groups such as addressing the Athenians on Mars Hill and the masses at Pentecost. They comforted friends in small groups such as the all-night vigil for Peter's prison release. They debated issues at the Jerusalem Council and at Cornelius' house. Hostile crowds were on their agenda from time to time—angry authorities, stonings, and trials. And they never passed up a chance to talk one-on-one. The Philippian jailer and the Ethiopian eunuch found their message quite persuasive. In all of these instances the Gospel message was proclaimed by disciples who followed the Master's methodology in word and deed.

In addition to the New Testament examples, the Old Testament prophets proclaimed their message with impact—from "billboards" (Hab. 2:2, TLB) to broken clay "jars" (Jer. 19:10-11, TLB). Finally, the Book of Proverbs contains numerous general truths about effective communication. For example, "He who speaks truth declares righteousness" (Prov. 12:17). There are also exhortations to listen well (Prov. 8:6, 33), seek counsel (Prov. 13:10), and use humor (Prov. 17:22).

With all this emphasis—by example and principle—in the Bible, certainly we can agree that the spoken word has power. That power can change our lives and the lives of our audiences—from the present day and for eternity.

The skills are yours for the practicing. Your effectiveness will increase as you are willing to invest the time and commitment to become a *confident communicator.*

Controlling Nervousness

"Stage fright" often begins long before we're on stage. For most, the condition overtakes us the moment we receive an invitation to make a presentation. And usually the longer we have to anticipate the big event, the more prolonged and severe the symptoms.

Sometimes our fears are rational and sometimes not. We fear that our subject or information is not quite what the audience expects, needs, or wants. We fear they'll attack us for our poor performance or challenge our credentials, asking a question we can't answer. Or we visualize ourselves making a misstatement or a grave omission of key information. And even if we know our subject well and are confident about our qualifications to speak on it, we feel that a poor performance may embarrass us.

Also, we fear the group will see our nervousness. If we have no other cause for fear, some of us worry that we won't have adequate time to prepare to do our usual good job or that some circumstance beyond our control (such as the AV equipment going berserk) will foul things up.

If any of these are your fears, you're in good company:

Sir Lawrence Olivier, Carol Burnett, Maureen Stapleton, Luciano Pavarotti, Willard Scott, and Johnny Carson all admit to fear before a performance. Political and business speakers also experience such anxiety because often they're presenting a script prepared by someone else to an audience ready to challenge their ideas.

> The idea is not to get rid of the butterflies in your stomach before a speech but rather to get them to fly in formation.
>
> —Anonymous

According to a study of 50,000 college students conducted at West Virginia University, researchers found that the typical person is "deathly afraid" of public speaking.

If you hear someone say he or she is not nervous before a presentation, you know you're talking to a boring speaker. If presenters don't have a certain amount of anxiety, their adrenalin will not be flowing to push them to a peak performance. They'll be too confident and relaxed to do their best job.

☞ 6. Fear Pushes to a Peak Performance

The secret of a great speaker is to perform despite the nervousness, actually making the nervousness a plus. Consider the tenseness and the extra adrenalin pumping through you as a catalyst to a great performance, the winning edge that you need to push you to excel.

Yes, you will feel on occasion that you've lost control of your body: rapid pulse, sweaty palms, dry mouth, buckling knees, muscle twitches, shortness of breath, quivering voice, butterflies in the stomach, queasiness.

But no matter how nervous you are, never tell the audience. If they sense your discomfort, they'll worry about you much like a parent does when a child mounts the school stage as Cinderella. Your admission to fear causes them to worry about your shaking hand when they should be listening to your words.

What's missing from our usual confident nature is feedback. In one-on-one conversation, we get immediate feedback from our listener—a raised eyebrow, a frown, an argument, a smile, a nod, a confirmation. In speaking before a group, we're lost without this immediate feedback. It's like stepping across a shallow river when you can't see the stones beneath the surface. You're a little nervous with each step until your toe touches the firm surface.

In controlling nervousness, keep in mind that you can't ever give in. Maybe you've found yourself in a situation similar to this one: In traveling all over the country, I often arrive in a strange city at night, rent a car, and drive to some remote hotel in the suburbs for the next day's conference. As I unload my luggage and walk from my car to the hotel room, I struggle to remain calm. Then as I get further away from the lights of the parking lot, my stride gets a little faster. If I see a strange person lurking along my path, my footsteps quicken as fear overtakes me. The last effort is a speedy push of my luggage cart inside the hotel door and a lunge for the night locks.

Once fear overtakes you, you're in trouble. Don't give in. Don't take that first step in permitting yourself to fall apart. Instead of thinking about yourself and how embarrassed you'll be, concentrate on your subject. Recall and rehearse your key points rather than your key obstacles.

Fear is a learned response. A two-year-old doesn't fear walking into the street until someone yanks her back and warns her of the danger. We learn that same fear of speaking before a group the first time a classmate stands up before the class to recite a poem, has a memory lapse, and gets flustered amid the snickers around the room. And if that fear is learned, it can be unlearned—or at least controlled.

One way to build your confidence is to remember that you were the one asked to give the presentation. At least someone believes you are capable and have the appropriate expertise on the subject. If others in the audience were more knowledgeable than you, they would have been asked to make the presentation.

☞ 7. Control Is the Secret

Sincere meditation gives strength. Remind yourself of the psalmist's words: "Whenever I am afraid, I will trust in You. In God (I will praise His Word), In God I have put my trust; I will not fear. What can flesh do to me?" (Ps. 56:3-4) Of course, most of us have much less to fear than physical harm. Our real fears more often revolve around fear of embarrassment.

With these "lesser" fears, another way I calm myself is to consider the whole experience in light of eternity. What's the worst that can happen? What will it all matter a year from now? In fact, if I goof, who will even remember it tomorrow? My little presentation, in the big scheme of things, is miniscule.

In fact, my husband often translates my irrational fears into a good laugh with his observations: "I can see it now in *USA TODAY*—Dianna Booher shows crooked slide with the colored edges creeping up because of the crummy overhead projector's surface. She was also wearing a navy-blue suit that wrinkled badly on the plane and. . . ." You get the picture. Learn to make fun of yourself. Put things into perspective.

Here are some more physical things you can do to get rid of the symptoms of nervousness:

● Take a few deep breaths and exhale slowly. (This forces the muscles to relax a bit, increases the flow of oxygen to the brain, and can lower the pulse rate.)

- Let all the muscles in your body go limp, then tense them, then let them go limp again.
- Clench your fists, then relax them.
- Let your arms dangle limply, rotate your wrists, then shake your fingers (like in the Hokey Pokey).
- Drop your jaw and wag it from side to side.
- Yawn. Drop your jaw, keeping your tongue flat against the bottom of your mouth. Suck in a few short breaths and you'll yawn yourself into relaxation.
- Roll your head or your shoulders or both.
- Go limp like a Raggedy Ann doll and then straighten up. Repeat.
- Select an object and stare at it for a long while, concentrating on relaxation.
- Take a brisk walk or jog before showing up at the event.

Select whichever mental or physical trick works best for you in a particular situation. The idea is to take yourself from terror, to fear, to tension, to merely "stimulation." Your stimulation will inspire or motivate your audience.

Focus your attention on what's going on around you or on your upcoming subject and away from yourself. Concentrate on your audience: How will your ideas help them improve their life or at least their knowledge base? Learn to appreciate the energy that tension creates; think of the swarm of butterflies in your stomach as a tank of creativity pushing outward to make you awesomely excellent. Feel passionate about your subject. Prepare well. Psyche yourself up for the positive results your presentation will bring.

☞ **8. Don't Let Fear Mean Mediocrity**

Don't let yourself be the "average" presenter, scared into conformity. Avoid the straight-laced performance—not too passionate, not too loud, not too flashy, not too funny, not too controversial, not too emotional, not too formal, not too informal, not too anything.

Instead of conforming to the mediocre, be yourself.

But be better than "natural." Be relaxed by being well prepared, but don't lose your tension. Emphasize your strengths so that your presentation memorably moves the audience to action or decision.

You may wonder if it is really possible for a shy person to be an excellent performer. After all, you can't just change an individual's personality with a snap of your fingers or a jab at the overhead projector. I have good news; it is possible. Stutterers often have no trouble singing. The lame may have no trouble swimming. The foreign-born can speak fluent English.

Moses provides a great example of an "average" speaker who became a powerfully persuasive leader as, with God's help, he petitioned Pharaoh and led the Israelites out of Egypt (see Exodus 6:28–7:7).

Larry Rogers, a lawyer friend of mine specializing in corporate finance, is another good example. Larry always dresses impeccably in a pinstriped suit and white shirt, but he more or less blends into the furniture (sorry, Larry) because he's so shy. Among our Bible study group, he nods and smiles when he enters the room, takes a seat, and never says another word unless spoken to.

Four years into this acquaintance, I was invited to conduct a seminar at Larry's company. The subject of public speaking and eloquence came up during our class discussion. Several of the participants commented that they wished they could be eloquent on their feet. Then one of the group turned to me and said, "Speaking of eloquence, you should hear one of our legal VPs here. He's fabulous. When he makes a presentation he has the audience eating out of his hand. He can think on his feet. His language and diction are flawless. His wit is charming. He's awesome." Several others chimed in.

"Oh, really," I responded. "Have I met him in an earlier class? Who is this?"

"Larry Rogers."

You too, no matter how shy, can blossom with the rest of the tips in this book.

Developing a Natural Delivery Style

2

Opinions vary widely about which is the most important to your success as a communicator—what you have to say or how you say it. Style or content. Well, in my experience they're equally important.

Great ideas zing my brain, and I love to play with new nuggets of information from knowledgeable speakers. But when I have to listen to a monotonous voice from a lifeless presenter, the fun evaporates quickly. Listening, rather than being a fun experience, suddenly becomes work.

On the other hand, I've listened to speakers with piles of pizzazz—humorous, graphic, animated, and smooth— and walked away thinking, "So what did she really say? What did she tell me that I haven't heard on every street corner and in every conference room? Where's the value?"

My conclusions are simply these: (1) When your ideas wear thin, quit entertaining and sit down. (2) When you run out of energy and animation, forget the ideas because the audience won't listen hard enough to hear them anyway.

☞ 9. Reveal Your Likable Personality and Attitude

Your delivery style is a direct reflection of your personality and attitude. To put it simply, people have to like you to believe you. Haven't you heard egotistical speakers who had a great message but lost your respect because of their arrogance? On the other hand, haven't you heard poor ramblers who had great difficulty organizing their thoughts and feelings but whose words moved you because you liked them personally? Think how much of former President Reagan's success can be attributed to the fact that the American public liked him. The media became fixed on that fact; almost every speech analysis during his eight years in office included the words "an extremely popular president."

We recently made a difficult "personality" versus "capability" choice in hiring a new trainer in our office. We interviewed a woman with a Ph.D. in journalism and eight years' experience in teaching adults technical writing. Our second applicant had a Master's degree and a likable personality. As a company, we would have been proud to present the Ph.D. to our clients—but only to the point where she began to offend. In our interview process, unfortunately, we detected a cynical, arrogant attitude that we feared would be abrasive to her audiences, our clients. People do not like to listen to people they don't like.

So what are those likable traits and attitudes? Following is an essential list to incorporate into your public speaking opportunities.

◆ Integrity
Audiences want to listen to someone they feel has the same integrity they have, someone who holds to the same moral values and to the same upbeat attitude about life. They want to believe you when you give facts and relate experiences.

◗ Genuineness

Audiences want to know that what they see is what they get. A few months ago, I heard a speaker at a convention make numerous offers to talk to participants after the session about their concerns and questions. He seemed genuinely interested in making himself available to anyone in the audience. However, when we saw him a few hours later and approached him to talk, his attitude was quiet different. In a brusque manner, he let us know quickly that he didn't have the time. You see, we weren't his prospective clients anymore; we were merely peers in a booth across the exhibit aisle.

Audiences sense genuineness. David A. Peoples, in his book *Presentations Plus,* puts it aptly when he characterizes audiences' attitudes this way: "Before I care how much you know, I want to know how much you care." They don't want you to hide who you are behind a "facts only" presentation—formal, emotionless, indifferent.

In general, be willing to share who you are with your audience, to laugh at your weaknesses, your mistakes, and your humanity.

◗ Enthusiasm

Relax and don't be afraid to show your attachment to your subject. "I'm excited about being here today" says good things to an audience. It generally means that you're confident that you have something of value to say and that you're prepared to state your case well. Boredom is contagious. Audiences get it from speakers who resist being "too emotional" about the ideas and outcome of their presentation.

Even the price of cabbage at your Loyola site can be exciting if you'll use a little creativity. Is the price higher or lower than last year? More profitable or less than the competitor's? Even the most mundane topics can be interesting to an audience if you show a little curiosity. If you need another push to show enthusiasm, consider the collective value of the time (salary per hour) of your audience. Is what you have to say worth $X per minute? Somebody evidently thought so in asking you to make the presentation. And that thought should shoot you through with enthusiasm for your subject.

Don't equate enthusiasm, however, with hysteria. Don't intimidate your audience by forcing them to raise their hands if they will contribute at least $X to your cause. So how much enthusiasm is too much? You have to be the judge. Let genuineness again be your guide. If you are emotional because you really feel conviction about what you're saying, then you're on solid ground with an audience. When you feel that you are faking enthusiasm, it's time to back off and cool down.

◗ Humility

Humility throws many beginning speakers because, on the one hand, audiences want you to be an expert and be knowledgeable about your subject and, on the other hand, want you not to be arrogant about your expertise. Ask yourself what's the right mix between expertise that establishes your credibility and humility that makes you likable rather than arrogant.

Yes, you do sometimes have to sell your own competence to speak on the subject. You can do this by selecting experiences, ideas, and illustrations that convey your range of expertise without sounding too egotistical or too understated.

Success rests on three things: *likableness, conviction,* and *competence.* But there are ways to show humility other than a modest presentation of your credentials. For example, make sure that you credit your sources of information or ideas borrowed from others.

And you can show humility on occasion by acknowledging your audience's expertise with a statement such as: "Frankly, I'm puzzled by the fact that I'm up in front of a group such as yours. Many of you have more experience in X than I. I only hope to share a different perspective on X for your consideration."

◗ "Us" Versus "You" Tone

Do you want a didactic tone or a "We're all in this together" tone? There are occasions for both. Listen to Peter's opening at Pentecost: "But Peter, standing up with the eleven, raised his voice and said to them, 'Men of Judea and all who dwell in Jerusalem, let this be known to you, and heed my words'" (Acts 2:14). Definitely, he followed this with a sermon. On other occasions, however, he sounded like just "one of the disciples."

You always have to decide what tone to take with your audience—that of expert, teacher, critic, peer, guide, or motivator.

All are appropriate on occasion, but choosing which to use is a strategic decision with any given audience. In general, adopt an "us" tone rather than a didactic one. In a contest of "eloquent and cold" versus "adequate and cordial," the latter always have the strongest impact.

◗ Goodwill and a Desire to Give Value

One of the biggest condemnations an audience can make when asked what a speaker had to say is, "Nothing much." Consider your presentation a commitment to give something of value to the audience. If you don't have the time to prepare or don't want to make the effort, then turn down the invitation to present.

That expectation of value is reflected in a question on an Exxon training evaluation form: "Did the instructor really seem to care that I learned something?" Along those same lines, the audience comments that mean the most to me are not those on eloquence, expertise, or enthusiasm but those from listeners who share something like, "What you said changed my life's direction." And no, I don't talk about spiritual concerns in my business presentations. But listeners who feel they have re-

ceived something valuable enough to change their career's direction or improve their commission check make
me feel that I've genuinely given value for my paycheck.

The audience has to believe that you have their best
interests at heart, that you have not arrived on the scene
to intentionally bore them, and that you are giving them
information to help, not hinder, them.

◆ Sense of Humor

You don't have to be a stand-up comic or even aim to
entertain your audience. Just adopt a light approach, an
attitude of spontaneity, a willingness to see humor in the
ordinary things that happen. Instead of griping when the
lights unexpectedly go out on your slide show, reward
everyone with an unscheduled break while you get things
under control. Instead of showing chagrin that the previous speaker stole your thunder, comment on his good
taste in choosing your favorite anecdote. Instead of being
nervous when you drop your note cards, quip, "I thought
I'd shuffle them halfway through and see if the ideas
would become more logical."

◆ Appropriate Dress

I'm not about to tell you how to dress; your dress must fit
your personality, the occasion, and your audience. But
don't leave any of those ingredients out of the decision.
Your dress tells your audience what you think of yourself
and what you think of them. Are they worth dressing up
for? Are you competent and worth looking at? Of course,
clothes are a part of body language to be used during the
presentation. Men sometimes like to loosen their ties and
roll up their sleeves to show openness and their commitment to their presentation.

Most audiences and speakers agree that it's better for
the speaker to be a little more formally dressed than the
audience out of respect for their importance and their
attention.

In summary, it is important to develop a likable personality and attitude. If you can win over your audience with your grace and charm, they are more likely to be receptive to your message. The spirit of this truth is well-exemplified in the Apostle Paul's proclamation, "I have become all things to all men, that I might by all means save some" (1 Cor. 8:22).

☞ **10. Presentation = Performance + Conversation**

After the attitude and personality check, your key delivery technique is your natural speaking style. To do this, catch yourself being natural with animation and enthusiasm about your subject and your purpose.

Performances focus on the *subject matter*—regardless of the audience's needs. Conversations focus on *what the other person needs and wants to hear.* You need both perspectives. Your style should be not a rambling discourse, which even makes for a bad conversation, but a planned, fresh style of talking one on one.

All of us act every day, according to Shakespeare: "All the world's a stage, and all the men and women in it merely players." We adapt our speaking somewhat when we're around others, getting a little more formal than when we sing to ourselves in the shower.

But good speakers try to be themselves—only a little better. In other words, if you don't normally pop off with witty lines, then don't try it in front of an audience. If you don't use slang and colloquialisms in everyday speech, don't try to use them in a presentation. Audiences, particularly young audiences, are sensitive to that kind of phoniness.

Of course, I'm not saying that conversation and speaking are exactly the same. There are differences. You feel more vulnerable in front of a group because several people have given you their attention rather than just a single individual. Because people have taken time away from their normal schedules, you feel more pressure to make what you say count—to be structured and logical. Finally, you may feel in limbo because your normal feedback pattern is altered. In natural conversation you see immediate reaction and receive feedback ("Oh, really?" "Then what?" "You're kidding!" "Why is that?") that helps guide and inspire you to continue. In speaking, you can't depend on those verbal clues to tell you how you're doing and if you're coming across okay.

The trick of effective speaking, then, is to take the best of both worlds—speaking and performing. Talk—only to a larger audience. Catch yourself in your natural animated and enthusiastic style. That's not to say that we're animated and enthusiastic every time we utter a word. You don't say, "The garbage needs to be taken out this morning" with the same fervor as, "I just won a trip to Europe!"

When I was coaching an instructor in improving the energy in her voice and body language, she kept telling me that she couldn't be more animated. She said it just "isn't me." Yet, when we finished the coaching session and talked personally for a few minutes, she unconsciously lapsed into her natural speaking style. While telling me about her dinner with an old friend, her voice grew livelier, her face glowed, her eyes smiled, and her hands and arms waved as she gestured appropriately with what she was saying.

"Stop. Freeze," I shouted at her. "Look at yourself in the mirror; let your voice echo in your mind."

She did so and, after a few interruptions that evening, began to realize that she was a naturally animated and enthusiastic person. Her stiff, before-a-group performance was really her "unnatural" self.

The idea is to *catch yourself being natural* while you're talking on the phone to a neighbor about the barking dogs outside, to the family about the day's experience with the auto mechanic, to a friend about a goof in forgetting someone's name, or to a colleague about a movie scene you thought hilarious. Simply learn to catch yourself in these situations; then feel what it feels like and hear what your voice sounds like. Copy that feeling and tone when you're speaking to a larger group.

That's the *natural* you, and that's your most effective delivery style. The animated and energetic person is who you are when you're with friends in a relaxed situation. The *unnatural* you is who you are when you become self-conscious in front of a group. So be yourself and simply talk to an audience larger than one.

☞ 11. Talk Rather Than Read

The reason we have so many deadly speeches and presentations is that many people choose to read to us—and read something that wasn't meant to be read aloud. The differences in spoken and written communication are enormous. For one, readers can always reread a document if they don't understand it the first time. In spoken communication the listener has only one chance to understand. A reader can stop, put the document aside, and consult a reference book for the meaning of a word. A listener can't. A reader can reread and untangle a long sentence; a listener can't. A reader can refresh himself on the key points by reviewing the structure of the document; a listener can't review unless a speaker helps with repetition and visuals.

Simply being aware of these differences between written and spoken language will make you more conscious of what it takes to explain a complex concept in an oral presentation.

♦ Use Simple Words and Short Sentences
If you use words that your audience does not understand they will stop listening. Or worse, they'll become angry, thinking that you are only trying to impress them, want to

make them feel ignorant, or didn't care enough to find out how much they knew about your subject. And all of these reactions are detrimental to your purposes.

Big words are not necessarily a sign of intelligence. The ability to make a complex subject understandable to the lay person is the mark of an effective communicator.

If you don't understand something, use longer words. Share the ignorance with your readers.

—Horton's Laws

Had President Bush told the American people that he wanted a "more benignant, more docile nation" rather than a "kinder, gentler nation," would he have carried half the country?

Prefer the familiar word to the unfamiliar: *unusual* instead of *anomalous; many* instead of *myriad; embarrassed* instead of *chagrined; cut* instead of *lacerated; rare* instead of *esoteric.*

Prefer the concrete to the abstract: *warehouse* instead of *facility; Chevy truck* instead of *vehicle.*

Prefer the short word to the long: *use* instead of *utilize; change* instead of *modification.* Don't let your education get in the way of your being an effective speaker. A large vocabulary is nice when you need it to understand someone else or to select the only word that really conveys your true meaning. Just don't show off your knowledge and confuse your audience.

Prefer short sentences to long ones: Long sentences lose listeners. Short ones are clearer and easier for you to deliver while still breathing naturally.

Prefer one strong word to several weak ones: *"We*

agree" instead of *"We are found to be in agreement with"; "He continued"* instead of *"He went on to say. . . ."*

Don't use words you can't pronounce. Someone in an audience once corrected my pronunciation of "subsidence" in such an embarrassing way that I'll never mispronounce it again. Lyndon Johnson's speech writers removed words that he found difficult to say. And I've found that to be the best solution for myself. In taping an audioseries with Nightingale-Conant, I learned that I simply can't pronounce the word *error;* now I remember to say *mistake.* Choosing a simpler, clearer word is always preferable to choosing one that you mumble, muffle, slur, or overarticulate to get exactly right. The simple word creates impact.

"Give me liberty or give me death."

—PATRICK HENRY

"I have a dream."

—MARTIN LUTHER KING

"Ask not what your country can do
for you; ask what you can do
for your country."

—JOHN F. KENNEDY

"Just say no."

—NANCY REAGAN

"A kinder, gentler nation."

—GEORGE BUSH

"I'd like to teach the world to sing
in perfect harmony."

—POPULAR SONG LYRIC

"Haste makes waste."

—FAMLIAR SAYING

"We have nothing to fear but fear itself."

—FRANKLIN ROOSEVELT

"I am the way, the truth, and the life."

—JESUS CHRIST

The simple word creates impact

◗ Use Specific, Vivid Language
Try to help your audience understand your message with graphic, vivid "picture" words that help them see and feel. Not "an angry individual," but "a yelling, freckle-faced teenager." Not "an orderly operation" but "a print-run where we made 428 copies without a single skipped page or ink smudge in the margins." Not "a growing concern to our profitability" but "in six months we'll be in the red by $30,000."

◗ Use the "You" Approach
Keep focused on your audience as if talking to them individually. Not "as this group is probably aware," but "as you are aware." Not "if management agrees," but "if we agree to work together."

◗ Omit Clichés of the Occasion
Avoid the worn, tired phrases that sound as though they were lifted from a book: "facing an important challenge"; "we welcome the opportunity"; "we must forge ahead"; "we are only as good as the decisions we make"; "he fought a hard fight." Such clichés sound foreign to the familiarity of everyday occasions.

◗ Use Colloquialisms and Slang When Appropriate
We dress differently on different occasions; we speak differently on occasion to create identification with our audience. "He informed us of his decision about the downsizing" is formal. "He laid it on the line about our jobs" is informal. Your use of formal or informal expressions should match the occasion.

◗ Avoid Poor Grammar
Proper grammar is still the mark of education in our society. Watch for incorrect use of pronouns such as "John and him went to the store." Watch for adjectives when you need adverbs: "He did good" when you mean "He

did well." Be careful about subject-verb agreement: "He don't have the proper identification" when you need "He doesn't have the proper identification." Avoid double negatives such as "The company doesn't have no inventory at this site" when you mean "The company doesn't have any inventory at this site."

At the risk of blowing my own horn here, I suggest you pick up a copy of my grammar book, *Good Grief, Good Grammar,* at your local bookstore. A humorous treatment of the most common grammatical errors, it's a do-it-yourself kit for those serious about correcting grammatical goofs common to public speakers.

☞ 12. Assume a Friendly Audience

With the assumption that everyone's out to catch you in an error or argue with you, you will feel nervous and may even sound hostile toward your audience.

In my own experience and that of many other professional speakers, audiences want you to do well. After all, they've taken time out of their schedules to hear you. They hope to gain something by the experience. And even if they were forced to hear you by a boss or a nagging spouse, they still will be pleasantly surprised that you gave them something of value or entertained them.

To reassure yourself that they are friendly and positive, arrive early and speak to people individually. Chat about the occasion, their trip to the site, what they do for a living, common acquaintances, anything that lets them see you as a nice person interested in them. Such chitchat also allows you to see them as familiar "friends" who'll welcome and benefit from what you have to say later.

If for some reason you don't have the opportunity to chitchat beforehand, you can do this in front of the group before you actually begin your presentation. Ask the audience if they're comfortable. Is the room too hot? Too dark? Ask your audience to applaud someone else who's had a great deal to do with the meeting details and planning. Compliment your audience on their effort to attend: "You must be the kind of people who care how the community youth spend their leisure time."

Even your body language conveys how you feel about your audience. If they're friendly, you tend to walk and stand closer to them. If you're afraid of them, you cloister yourself behind a podium or table and lean away.

Relate to those sitting closest to you at first. In general, the people who choose to sit closest to the speaker perceive the session to be of value and want to be up front so they won't miss anything. Or someone has already told them that you, or your message, or both are terrific and they're eager to hang on every word. Concentrate on those friendly faces at the beginning of your presentation, and then spread your smile and attention to those further back as you warm up.

Finally, don't let yourself be discouraged by frowns or silences. Silence can mean deep thought and agreement as often as it does boredom. I remember having an engineer in an audience whom I worried about from the opening moments. When she entered, she spoke to no one and barely made eye contact with me or anyone else the rest of the morning. She propped her chin in her hand and doodled on a scratch pad throughout the presentation. I tried every technique I could muster to involve her, to raise a smile, to get some sort of sign that she was interested or following anything I said. Finally, assuming her to be a lost cause, I gave up. Imagine my surprise when I later read her evaluation of the session: "Absolutely the best presentation I've ever attended. Should be required for every engineer in the company."

So much for reading body language. Yes, you must be sensitive to the body language of your audience, but at the least, you can generally assume that your audience will listen respectfully. At best, they will agree with what you have to say. With this assumption your delivery will sound relaxed and upbeat.

☞ **13.** **Pay Attention to Your Own Body Language**

Only 7 percent of our message comes from our words. That's right, according to Albert Mehrabian whose often-cited study shows that audiences perceive us in three ways: 55 percent visually, 38 percent vocally, and only 7 percent verbally.

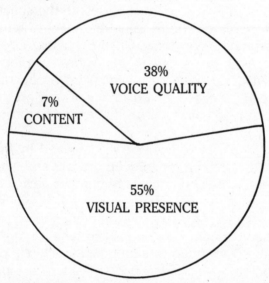

Your message depends on much more than your words.

Think of the implications. That means that the way you approach the group, your dress, your gestures, your posture, your smile, and your eye contact determine 55 percent of the impact you have.

▶ **Eye Contact**
Eye contact, or the lack thereof, is the most noticeable mannerism. Eye contact makes it extremely difficult to

turn away from someone who is looking at you. When you've made eye contact with someone in your audience, you've established a bond. You've signaled your interest in that person and your sincerity in what you're saying. In fact, we often hear it said, "I bet he couldn't look you in the eye and say that." Or, "She was giving me the evil eye when I said that."

Someone has said, "Eyes are the windows of the soul," and that's especially true for the speaker. Lovers spend hours staring into each other's eyes to share the feelings words can't express. Enemies watch their opponents' eyes to determine their next move. Tackles watch the quarterback's eyes to avoid the fake. Negotiating teams seat themselves around a table to interpret the reactions to offered terms that are reflected in their opponents' eyes. Using the eyes effectively is crucial to success.

There are a few don'ts of eye contact too. Don't stare at one or two people or at a spot in the back of the room. Don't flit your eyes around the room as if they're afraid to land on anyone's face. Don't stare at your notes, the table, or the AV equipment. Don't read from a script so that you can offer only momentary glances between thoughts. Don't look around, through, or over your listeners' heads. Finally, don't stand so far away from your audience that they can't see your eyes even when you're looking at them.

Now the do's. Do glance around from time to time and sweep in the view of everyone. You may face certain sections of the room for one complete point before moving to the next. Do hold your eyes on different individuals to establish personal contact. Let your eyes fall on that individual, hold that contact, make your point, then move to the next pair of eyes.

Eye contact is a form of paragraphing. You deliver a point, a phrase, a punchline, an illustration to one person, then lift your eyes and move to the next person to deliver the next point. One or two sentences delivered to each person establishes a strong bond of intimacy with your listeners as individuals.

▶ Gestures and Mannerisms

Gestures and mannerisms either support or discredit what you say. They can convince your audience of your sincerity or antagonize them. Imagine yourself in an airport with conversations going on all around and you are engaged in a farewell to a friend. All of a sudden, the man and woman sitting next to you begin to flail their arms dramatically, their fingers punching the air with urgency. Immediately, your attention is diverted from your own conversation to this couple. Why did their words not disturb you while their gestures did? That's the power of gestures and mannerisms; often they speak louder than words.

You may be completely serious about and confident with what you have to say, but the audience may perceive you to be insincere because of poor eye contact, a slouched posture, a bored expression, or limp arm gestures.

The following list of the most common gestures and mannerisms should increase your awareness of your own body language.

Dictatorial:
- crossed arms
- hands on hips
- hands behind back
- hands in steeple position
- pounding fist
- pointing index finger
- karate chops in the air

Openness to Audience:
- open palms upward
- large, above-the-waist arm gestures

- removing your glasses
- moving to the front of the podium
- stepping off the platform
- walking toward and into the audience
- leaning forward on your toes or the edge of your chair
- hand-to-face gestures
- unbuttoned coat or shirt collar, loose tie
- chin tilted to the side

Insecurity/Nervousness:
- gripping the lectern or AV equipment
- chewing objects such as pencil erasers
- biting fingernails
- biting lips
- continual throat clearing
- hands in pockets
- hands covering mouth
- clenched fists
- no eye contact
- jingling keys or money in pocket
- pulling off glasses and replacing them
- strumming fingers
- touching ears
- playing with hair, mustache, or beard
- twisting rings or other jewelry
- rocking back and forth or from side to side
- tossing chalk, marker, or pointer in air
- rubbing hand across forehead and through hair
- rubbing back of neck

Emphasis:
- underscoring a point on the visual
- large arm movements from the shoulder
- dramatic pauses
- lifted eyebrows
- head poised in reflective tilt

- bouncing gently on toes
- animated facial expression

Whatever the gestures, they serve three main purposes: to release your own nervous tension, to gain and hold the audience's attention, and to underscore your message.

Appropriateness is also paramount. With an inspiring message to motivate an audience to action, full-blown gestures, excited movement, and a loud voice are natural and supportive. With a group of elder statesmen, you may want to replace the rah-rah motions with long eye contact, deliberate gestures, and a determined squint in your eye. In a small room, large gestures may make you feel like an elephant in a china shop. In a large room, small gestures will make you look like a bewildered child.

To sum up, negative gestures and mannerisms include both a slouched posture and a rigid stance with no movement; limp, small hand gestures; fixation in playing with clothes and objects; word fillers such as *aahh*'s and *uh*'s.

Positive gestures include a comfortable posture; big, open gestures; an animated facial expression; and effective silences rather than word fillers.

So how do you break the bad habits and form new ones? With a conscious effort. For example, clap your hands. Now cross your hands and clap them again the opposite way. Feels awkward, right? Any conscious change you make will seem awkward, but that doesn't mean it will look awkward to your audience. Here are a few pointers in improving your gestures and mannerisms.

First of all, simply look at yourself in the mirror and feel how it feels to stand with your hands at your side or with your elbows slightly bent. It may feel awkward, but it doesn't look awkward. Just get used to the feel so you can relax with it in front of a group.

Try simply speaking loudly. The louder you talk, the more natural it will be to use gestures. Consider the last argument you had with a family member—waving arms, scrunched-up mouth, wagging head. It's difficult to use big, open gestures with a tiny voice, isn't it? The reverse also works. Raising the volume to an appropriate level will usually improve your gesturing in a natural way.

If you've taken to heart earlier advice about being conversational, most of your gestures will be naturally appropriate and effective. The intellectual and emotional energy from gut level reflects the feelings you have about your subject. It will come out naturally through your body if you let it. The real secret is to catch yourself being natural, only in front of a group.

▶ Movement

Consider use of your physical space as part of your presentation. Walking into your audience shows them you're not afraid to look them in the eye or answer their questions. Be careful about setting up artificial barriers such as a podium, table, or raised platform away from the front row of your audience.

Physical closeness lends intimacy to your talk. Such proximity also helps you keep the attention of your audience. It's difficult to fall asleep if the speaker is only three feet away from your chair or may reach out to make a note on your legal pad on the table in front of you.

Finally, physically moving about in your audience's space helps control any problems or distractions. For example, a side conversation between two people in the meeting can be immediately stopped by just casually strolling toward that side of the room. The talkers feel all eyes following you, and they don't want to be caught in the spotlight talking.

Physical closeness can also stop an individual in the audience from dominating a discussion. In such a situation, casually stroll toward that dominating person, turn your back and face away from him to deliver your next point or ask your next question. You have physically closed him off, and he will hold his tongue until you "give him permission" again by facing him.

Eye contact, gestures, mannerisms, and use of physical space either support or detract from your words.

☞ 14. Modulate Your Voice

Let's consider that other 38 percent of your message—the impact of the voice. Four things constitute the impact of your voice: volume, pitch, quality, and pace.

♦ Volume

Volume is the loudness of your voice. In our society, little girls are taught that loud voices are not feminine while boys learn no such inhibitions. As a result, women often have problems with speaking loudly enough. In today's business arena, wimpy voices get little attention. Consider the extreme. When someone shouts, everyone turns to look—regardless of what's being said. Volume gets attention.

William T. Brooks, writing in *High Impact Public Speaking,* recounts a widely circulated story about evangelist Billy Sunday, who moved large crowds to commitment with his message. Sunday often wrote notes to himself in his script margins on delivery techniques. A biographer looking through his outlines after his death found this frequent notation: "Shout loud! This is a weak point!"

Regardless of our opinion of his technique, we do know Billy Sunday had power with audiences. The best of all worlds is to have power with both your voice and your message.

Just remember that your voice always sounds louder to you than to anyone else. Take other people's word for it when they say you need to learn to speak up. Also remember that your voice is an instrument; it needs to be warmed up for best use or it will creak and crack at the beginning of your presentation. If you'll warm up with a high volume as if projecting to those in the back of the room, your volume will improve your voice quality also.

Volume adds spice to your voice; it commands or loses the attention of your listeners.

.

♦ Pitch

Pitch is the measurement of the "highness" or "lowness" of your voice. Pitch is largely determined by the amount of tension or relaxation in the vocal cords. So when you're under stress, you may sound higher pitched. When you're relaxed, you'll have a naturally lower pitch.

You want to aim at a lower pitch. Authoritative voice tones are low and calm, not high and tense. Inflection is a pitch change—from "please stop" screeched at an assailant to "please stop" echoed to a subordinate using the copy machine. A lower pitch conveys power, authority, and confidence. A high pitch reveals insecurity and nervousness.

♦ Quality

Quality involves such things as a breathy sound, a tense harshness, hoarseness, nasal tones, or a deep resonating solemn sound. Quality is also measured by weaknesses such as slurring of words, articulating certain sounds, accents, and so forth. You can put a smile or anger in your tone. Quality is very subjective and is determined by the listener.

Work at putting a smile in your tone. Nervous speakers often get so caught up in content that they sound and look much too serious for the occasion. I've seen presenters explain the procedures for completing an exercise in as solemn a fashion as if giving a eulogy. The idea is to match your voice quality with your content.

Also, you'll want to make sure you control your breath enough to complete each sentence briskly, rather than having your words drop off at the end. Breath control also allows you to stress the most important words and downplay the least important.

Finally, pay attention to clear articulation, remembering not to drop the final syllable off words (*eatin'* versus *eating*), and giving full value to all the sounds in the words.

◗ Pace

Pace is the rate of speaking—either slowly or quickly. Neither extreme is correct, but you should know the pros and cons of both a fast and a slow pace to determine the effect you want. A fast rate shows excitement and energy and commands attention so that listeners do not miss what you say. Speak too quickly, however, and your listeners may have difficulty understanding your words.

A slow speaking rate adds drama and emphasizes key points. It gives listeners time to reflect on what you say. Speaking too slowly, however, may cause listeners' minds to wander or convey the impression that you don't know what's coming next or don't really have much information to give. Because we listen four times as fast as we speak, a slow speed may lose your audience entirely.

Again, variety is the key. For serious information, you should speak a bit slower; for a humorous story, a bit faster. For large audiences speak slowly enough for your sound and movements to create impact on the back row. For small, intimate groups you should speed up a little.

To add emphasis, vary any of these: volume, pitch, quality, or pace. A loud statement followed by a soft one. A deep solemn pronouncement followed by a high-pitched plea for help. A deep, resonant, precise articulation of the fourth-quarter profits followed by a slangy conclusion, "There ain't nothin' doin'." A quickly delivered rah-rah for the sales team, followed by a slow sincere thank you for their efforts.

To top off your skillful voice techniques, remember the use of silences. Never be afraid of silences. Used effectively, they punctuate your meaning. They say to the audience, "Now, just pause and think of that." Or, "Sit up and take notice of this next point—it's a biggy." Silences also give your audience breathing room between ideas.

Silences are also effective ways to involve your audience in introspection. Ask a rhetorical question and then pause, giving them a chance to pose their own answer before you rush ahead with yours.

Speeches without pauses cause ideas to run together and make it difficult for listeners to distinguish between major and minor ideas.

Keep in mind that your voice is the method of your message. It has to be there but should not call attention to itself. If any of these aspects—volume, pitch, quality, or pace—call attention away from your message, your voice has become a liability rather than an asset.

☞ 15. Take Stage

There should be no doubt when you've taken control of the meeting or discussion. Think of your audience as attendees at an amusement park. They've all assembled and climbed on the ferris wheel, and you're the one to turn the switch and send them swirling. If you never get going, your riders just sit there mentally and physically frustrated.

Power or intensity is the voltage that your presence brings to the scene. Audiences need to feel it; they anticipate it and respond to it. Jesus had that intensity when He spoke "as one having authority" (Mark 1:22). When He entered a room, crowds hushed to hear His message. His presence even kept the attention of hot, tired audiences gathered on a hillside. His body language and eyes showed both compassion and, at times, condemnation as He upbraided the hypocritical Pharisees. Definitely, He had control and stage presence as He scolded the money changers and drove them from the temple (Matt. 21:12-13).

So how do you command attention from the very beginning? You do it with your posture and body language, your movement toward the front of the group, and your opening remarks.

First, approach the front with deliberate, purposeful steps rather than as if you were being dragged forward against your will. Don't imitate the approach of the "volunteer" whose friends have just pushed her up on stage to be the brunt of some comedian's joke. Stand with your weight evenly on both feet, not slumped to the side or leaning against a table or podium. Take a moment to get your bearings. Place any notes or visuals in front of you. Adjust the equipment you plan to use. Then gaze out at your audience and pause. Greet them and then respond to your introduction, acknowledge the occasion, or simply begin your presentation.

These opening few seconds are crucial—this is when your audience takes stock of you and decides whether you're worth listening to. When you open your mouth, half your opportunity to make a good impression is already gone.

And remember that your audience may even be watching you before you "take stage." While you're still awaiting your time in the limelight, don't fidget with your clothes, pat your hair into place, shuffle through your notes, or re-sort your visuals. Such activity connotes a lack of interest in and respect for the current proceedings, as if you're waiting for the most important event— you—to begin.

If an introducer is particularly flowery, avoid the eyes of the audience and simply smile at the introducer as if acknowledging that the words are a little too much. Your first eye contact with the audience should be when you stand up to face them.

Another big part of taking stage is your opening remarks—those made before your real presentation material. For example, acknowledging your introduction or the occasion. Or complimenting the audience. Or verifying their comfort before you begin. Above all, avoid the opening clichés that mark you as insincere or as a lazy thinker, or both.

Thank you, John Smith. Ladies and Gentlemen. Members of the committee. Thank you for that fine introduction. I also appreciate your invitation and let me say how happy I am to be with you on this auspicious occasion in your wonderful organization. I'm also pleased that you included me in that fine meal.

Avoid opening clichés

Instead of the formal clichés, start fresh. Say what's on your mind and say it sincerely. "Thank you for that introduction" is adequate and appropriate on occasion. You may add why you were asked to be on the program or make the presentation, compliment the audience, mention the importance of the subject matter, or comment on your state of mind or your personality and how that relates to the occasion, subject, or audience. If you're particularly quick-witted, you may refer to some earlier incident, joke, or occurrence in the program that will tie into your introductory remarks. Such an impromptu comment always impresses your audience with your wit, freshness, and openness in departing from "scripted" lines.

Take charge totally with posture, body language, attentive gaze to the audience, voice tone, and fresh comments. Don't be tentative in purpose. Project an attitude of anticipation and eagerness. Look confident. Let the audience know that you have come to give them value and you are about to unleash many benefits to them if they'll just listen up.

☞ 16. Involve Your Audience

Somehow you must create audience participation. Involvement may be an opinion poll, a show of hands to agree or disagree, games or activities, or simply a question — games or activities, or simply a question — rhetorical or otherwise. Jesus often presented His concepts with such questions: "But who do you say that I am?" (Luke 9:20) "Simon, son of Jonah, do you love Me more than these?" (John 21:15) "Whose image and inscription is this?" (Matt. 22:20) The listeners' answers led to further learning and often to personal commitment. Never underestimate the power of personally involving your audience in your presentation through such involvement techniques.

☞ 17. End with Impact

Don't whimper to a close. We've all heard speakers who mumble their last lines as they begin to shuffle together notes and visuals and clutch them to their body. "I guess that's about all I have. Any questions?" they add as an afterthought, never making eye contact to welcome any. Then they slink back to their seats, averting their eyes until someone else is on the spot and assumes control of the meeting.

You can do much better. First, to end with impact, you need to leave your audience with a dramatic closing line (tips on doing that come in part 3). Second, stop when you're finished. No, that's not the same thing. Some speakers have a habit of ending with their prepared strong closing line and then mumbling on, re-explaining, adding, fumbling to make the same points in an anticlimactic way.

Abe Lincoln once remarked: "He can compress the most words into the smallest idea of any man I ever met."

Even the writer of Ecclesiastes comments on the phenomenon: "Do not be rash with your mouth. . . . For God is in heaven. . . . Therefore let your words be few" (Ecc. 5:2). To say more than needs to be said is a great mistake. Remember that the Lord's Prayer is only 71 words, the Ten Commandments 297 words, and the Gettysburg Address (the most quoted speech in history) only 271 words. You've probably discovered that those who have the most significant message usually deliver it with the fewest words.

When your idea runs its course, simply stop. Add nothing. Don't mumble. Smile and physically "close up shop." Pause and gaze at your audience with a last moment of confidence that they'll agree with what you've just said. Then pick up your notes and walk away in the same deliberate and purposeful way you approached the group.

Take your ending time as seriously as you expect airlines to. Land on time and with precision.

To sum up: Give attention to attitude and personality traits that come through to your audience—integrity, genuineness, enthusiasm, humility, a "We're in this together" tone, goodwill and a desire to give value, a sense of humor, and appropriate dress.

To develop a natural delivery, make your presentation both a *performance* and a *conversation:* Talk rather than read. Use simple words and short sentences. Use specific, vivid language. Use the "you" approach. Omit clichés. Use colloquialisms and slang when appropriate, but avoid poor grammar.

Assume a friendly audience. Pay attention to your own body language. Add variety in your voice—volume, pitch, quality, and pace. Take stage. Involve your audience. And finally, end with impact.

Planning and Organizing Your Message

3

Here's a bird's-eye view of what you'll need to do to prepare for any given speech:

- Determine the purpose of your presentation.
- Analyze your audience.
- Gather your information.
- Compose a one-sentence overview of your main idea to serve as a road map.
- Outline your information, including a good opening, transitions between key points, and a closing.
- Write a first draft of the script (optional).
- Edit and polish it (optional).
- Time your script or outlined presentation.
- Prepare your visuals.
- Prepare your notes or outline for delivery.
- Practice.
- Destroy your script and deliver your message.

How necessary is all this preparation? Why not just "wing it," as the less prepared say? Consider our model. Jesus Christ spent thirty years of His life preparing for His ministry and only three years teaching and preaching. His life's mission, of course, bore out the need for that intensive preparation. But even if our mission is less encompassing, it will require some preparation. As you plan your speaking project, determine your goal and taper your preparation time accordingly.

Just as it is with Olympic performances, a great deal of work must go into the presentation before you ever appear in front of the group. The necessity for knowing where you're going is just as strategic in communication as it is in the sports arena.

☞ 18. Determining Your Purpose

Simply by their presence, your audience has made a commitment to hear you. Either the group needs your advice, your information, or your inspiration—or all three. Try to think of your presentation as a product or service that must fill a niche market. Just as advertisers do before they launch a new ad campaign, consider your audience carefully.

Ask yourself: "Why *me?*"

Why have you been chosen to present this information or message? What specific qualities or credentials do you have? That uniqueness will give you a big clue as to what strengths you can bring to the talk. For example, were you particularly close to a business associate so that you can add emotional depth to his farewell address? Are you the specialist who did the research on a project and can answer questions more authoritatively than anyone else? Are you a recognized authority in a certain subject so that your name adds credibility to already accepted ideas? Have you had a tragic event in your life and been comforted by your faith in Christ so that others can gain real hope by hearing of your experience?

Ask yourself: "Why *them?*"

Why has the group assembled to hear *you?* Did their boss, spouse, or child "request" them to attend? Do they have a personal interest in you? Do they have an interest in the subject? Or do they want to hear you so they can contradict you and subvert your efforts and ideas? Did they come to hear someone else and you happen to be on the program also? Is this their monthly organizational meeting and they always show up, no matter what? An honest answer to these questions can give you essential help with what kind of opening remarks, what tone, and what order for presenting your ideas should be incorporated into your speech.

For example, Lee Iacocca did a great deal of audience analysis while he prepared his pitch to Congress for the unprecedented loan to bail out Chrysler's bankruptcy. In his book, *The Manager's Complete Guide to Speech Writing,* speechwriter Burton Kaplan notes Iacocca's intense focus on the mood and self-interest of his audience. He was primarily addressing Congress, but, secondarily, he had to convince taxpayers, the United Auto Workers, and general car buyers. The Treasury Department had estimated that if Chrysler collapsed, the cost would be $2.7 billion during the first year in unemployment insurance and welfare paid to the laid-off workers. After carefully analyzing the probable reactions, Iacocca put it this way: "You guys have a choice. Do you want to pay the $2.7 billion now, or do you want to guarantee a loan of half that amount with a good chance of getting it all back? You can pay now or you can pay later."

Specifically and with care determine: "Why me? Why them? For what purpose? What do I want them to know, decide, believe, feel, or do as a result of my presentation?"

☞ 19. Analyzing Your Audience

After you've determined your purpose, you want to analyze your audience so that your purpose will seem immediate to them. For some presentations, your purpose is already specific to the audience: "I want the people of this subdivision to change the restrictions on garbage collection."

But for other occasions, your general purpose (to get people to contribute money to the community youth programs) may need to be focused more specifically (to get parishioners of Central Christian Church to give money to the Summer Youth Mission Project).

The principle is this: If you're a single adult and read a news story about a teenager killed on a motorcycle because he wasn't wearing a safety helmet, you may feel sorry, shake your head, and continue to read. But if you just bought your own eighteen-year-old a motorcycle and had an argument with him about wearing a safety helmet, then you're going to tune in a little closer to the safety statistics to find out how you can convince your son to cooperate with the law.

Immediacy is the key.

Meeting planners calling to book speakers for their corporate audiences comment more and more frequently: "We want someone who can get specific on a topic. We want to walk away from the meeting with specific how-to's—not just an inspirational hodgepodge."

I think you'll find that true of most audiences—professional groups wanting answers about money management or marital problems, or your community committee wanting to prevent the use of drugs in the neighborhood.

Therefore, get specific. What are their needs and wants? Do you want to inform, persuade, teach, inspire, or entertain?

▶ What Do You Need to Know?
For starters, here are some key questions that will need to be answered for various occasions:
- What is the age, sex, race, religion, or political bent of the audience?
- What is the proportion of men to women?
- What is their educational background?

- What is their occupation?
- What is their work experience—technical or non-technical?
- What is their income level?
- What do the individuals' lifestyles have in common?
- What organizations do they belong to?
- What is their motivation for hearing the presentation?
- What are their prejudices and biases about this subject?
- What are the current problems or challenges of this group?
- What are their goals and wants?
- What are the significant events related to this meeting, corporation, city, or organization?
- Are there any taboo subjects or issues?
- Will they appreciate humor or is this a solemn occasion?
- What is their style of learning—seeing, hearing, or doing?
- What are their attitudes about attending your presentation? Passive? Put upon? Competitive with you or each other? Unified with you and the others in their group? Manipulated for having to attend or participate in any way? Resistant to your ideas and philosophy? Afraid they can't master what you're saying? Challenged to adopt your ideas? Eager to try out your information? Uncomfortable with the seating arrangement?
- How many people will be in the audience? (This will determine your use of visuals, room arrangement, and interaction possibilities.)
- What is the layout of the room and can it be altered?
- Will there be food and beverages served before, during, or after?
- How will the audience be dressed?
- What have other speakers on the program (or in past) addressed and what was the audience reaction?
- What is the theme of the meeting?

- Will there be a question-and-answer period?
- Will there be any special VIPs, guests, or press present?

▶ How Do You Get Information?

You can start with the person who invited you to make the presentation. And be specific. Not: "Could you tell me a little about the group?" But: "What specific details can you give me about the group that will help me customize my comments to the exact needs and moods of the audience?" And then be ready with your written list of questions, if necessary.

But don't stop with that meeting planner. I've often discovered that the meeting planner knew very little about the audience or had a totally opposite view of the purpose of the meeting as well as the interest and knowledge level of those attending.

Go to members or prospective members of the audience to ask the same questions. Your methods may be formal or informal, but you need such information from all groups—business associates or Bible study group members. You can phone a select few ahead of time, survey all the members of the group with a formal questionnaire, or stand at the front door and chitchat as they arrive.

Other sources for general information will be literature published by the group or at least offered by their organization, copies of past program bulletins and evaluations, and "hearsay" about reactions to past meetings.

In addition to these efforts in analyzing your audience, keep in mind that all audiences have a life and personality of their own. The chemistry of these unique individuals can turn them into a supportive, challenged audience that hangs on every word leaving your lips. Or, the combination of personalities can make them conform to the passivity of a few leaders. Despite this last-minute phenomenon of synergy, do all you can to know all you can about the group.

☞ **20.** **Narrowing Your Ideas to Key Points**

Contrary to what you may think, the most frequent problem will be narrowing your ideas to a few good points rather than generating enough ideas. For most business occasions your key points are pretty well assumed by the purpose of the meeting.

Just remember that in these days of thirty-second commercials, 200-word newspaper fillers, one-sentence magazine blurbs, one-hour photos, one-hour cleaning, and thirty-minute pizza deliveries, your audience appreciates brevity.

Corporate pocketbooks do as well. Figure the salaries of those gathered to hear you, and ask yourself if each point is worth $X per minute.

☞ **21.** **Gathering Your Information and Ideas**

The task is much easier if you have an ongoing file of notes and clippings. Even if you're not a professional speaker on the lecture circuit, you probably have ongoing personal and career interests in certain subjects. Keep files of jokes, quotes, statistics, and anecdotes about your subject. Jot the source in the margin of the clipping, and toss it into the file.

Another source is your personal experience. Cull your own background for anecdotes, overheard conversations, reactions to problems, feelings, and moods that will underscore the key points you want to make in your presentation. Many people keep a journal of intriguing experiences, conversations, or happenings they've witnessed. You never know when one will be the exact illustration you need to make your point and win audience identification.

Then go to your friends and acquaintances and probe their memories for similar experiences or personal information. You'd be surprised how many anecdotes you can gather to reinforce your points if you just toss out your subject around the lunch table.

Finally, ask yourself what experts would know a certain fact, statistic, or situation. If you need to know the average shoe size sold to women, ask yourself who would have reason to know that. Shoe manufacturers or retail stores? If you need to know the number of abortions performed in the U.S. last year, ask yourself who would know. The HEW? The local abortion clinic? The local anti-abortion agencies? The school counselor? Call the library or a local university and get permission to quote a professor or a published source. Whatever your subject or need, some expert will know.

☞ **22. Avoiding Pitfalls in Preplanning**

Now that you have a fix on your audience and have gathered information on your subject, you're ready to organize the ideas into some structure. As you do, keep these guidelines in mind:

● Be wary about unsourced facts in print and on TV. If your whole point rests on a certain fact, check it from more than one source.

● Attribute quotes to the correct source. During my research of another subject, I found a particular Pascal (true source) quote attributed to no less than four other authors—Teddy Roosevelt, Andrew Jackson, Mark Twain, and Winston Churchill. Reference books are highly reliable. Memories aren't.

● Don't grab an exceptional situation and use it to "prove" your key point.

● Avoid sweeping generalizations of unsupported opinions.

● Don't take things out of context. The temptation is great to grab a key story or comment from a university professor, an author, or another recognized expert and fill in with a lot of assumptions. It's quite embarrassing when someone in your audience brings to your attention the fact that the expert you quoted actually supports the opposing idea.

● State your assumptions up front.

● Consider the validity of other positions on an issue— even if you don't present the opposing views, you'll have a more thorough and fair analysis of the subject.

If this sounds like work, it *is* trouble to double-check. But you have responsibilities and motivations to put in the extra time to be credible. One is Philippians 4:8: "Finally, brethren, whatever things are true, whatever things are noble, whatever things are just, whatever things are pure, whatever things are lovely, whatever things are of good report, if there is any virtue and if there is anything praiseworthy—meditate on these things." This should be all the incentive you need as a Christian. As a speaker, you are morally obligated to present the truth without deception.

A second (pragmatic) consideration is the embarrassment you will feel when a member of your audience calls your error to light.

☞ **23. Composing a Brief Overview**

The one-sentence overview serves as your road map. It combines your purpose, your message to your audience, and what you want the audience to do as a result of your presentation.

For example: "Our records-storage center has reached capacity. This warehouse storage costs us approximately $70,000 annually to house useless information. I recommend we revise our records-retention schedules, purge our current files, terminate our lease on the warehouse site, and begin a paperwork-reduction campaign. Within three years, I estimate we can reduce our paperwork costs by $1.8 million. I need your approval to implement these changes."

With such a comprehensive road map at the beginning, your presentation practically composes itself. In the above example, you immediately see the key supporting points you'll need: (1) current situation of waste and cost; (2) records-retention schedules, current and proposed; (3) how-to's of purging current files; (4) details of terminating lease; (5) steps and cost and how-to's of paperwork-reduction campaign; (6) estimation of savings; (7) approvals needed.

Composing such a succinct overview is *the single most important thing* you can do to ensure an effective presentation. Half the preparation is over at this point.

☞ 24. Structuring an Opening, Body, and Closing

The next step is to structure your ideas. Jot down the key points you already have in mind to support your message statement. Then list questions your audience will have about the subject. Lay the notes aside for a few days and let your subconscious mull over the ideas. As you come up with subpoints, additional illustrations, and tidbits, throw them into the pile with the first notes. When you're ready to do a formal outline of your ideas, retrieve the file and sort the ideas into some logical order (as explained in the next section). Discard what doesn't make sense now that the air has cleared. Write out a formal outline under these categories: opening, body, closing.

Three more things before you take off: tone, title, and timing.

☞ 25. Determining the Proper Tone

Do you want to be formal? Warm and witty? Light? Humorous? Informative? Persuasive? Entertaining? Your decision here will affect your word choice, your anecdotes, and even your key points and supporting details.

Discard any information that will lead to an improper tone.

☞ 26. Selecting a Title

Business presentations often require no title. In other settings, the title is often the audience's best indication of how they should react to your presentation. The title usually tells them whether the talk is light or serious, informative or merely entertaining. Titles can provoke your audience into adopting an attitude, question their perspective, challenge an assumption, predict results or the future.

Titles can play on a well-known quote, paraphrase a cliché or famous title, or simply describe a topic in a straightforward way. You may want your title to raise curiosity or to be informative. Whatever title you choose, it should do two things: get attention and describe your subject accurately. You don't want your audience to be disappointed because they misunderstood what you were going to speak about.

Your title may change as you develop your presentation, but take a stab at it in the planning stage so that you can refer to it like a road map for the focal message and the overall tone.

☞ 27. Planning Your Timing

You don't want an introduction that lasts ten minutes when the total speech is only twenty minutes. Keep proportion of the three parts (opening, body, closing) in mind. For an hour's presentation, a five- to ten-minute introduction may be appropriate. For a two-minute farewell to a colleague, you don't want to spend one minute telling why you were chosen to make the presentation. This timing issue also applies to key points in your presentation.

Time equals importance. Make sure each point gets the time it deserves—no more and no less.

Whatever happens, you don't want someone to announce that your time is up when you're only on the second of five points. The audience's apprehension grows along with yours.

"A multiplicity of words indicates poverty of thought."

"No speech is entirely bad if it's short enough."

"Too many people run out of ideas long before they run out of words."

—E.C. McKenzie

Timing is crucial.

The Genesis account of creation is told in only 400 words. The Lord's Prayer provided our model in only 56 words. Plan your speech accordingly in light of its importance to your audience.

☞ 28. The "Opening to the Opening"

Now that you have planned the title, the tone, and the timing, organize your ideas into a more cohesive whole: an opening, a body, and a closing.

First, consider the two kinds of openings. I call one the "opening to the opening." That is, the first opening is more or less reacting to or commenting on the occasion itself, whereas the second is introducing your topic. Occasionally, they can be smoothly combined.

Primarily, the opening must get attention. TV networks

spend enormous amounts of money on engaging titles, splashy music, and intriguing storyline blurbs to keep you tuned in for the upcoming TV show. Your own crafted introduction will either gain or lose your audience.

The opening must also establish rapport with the audience. They have to want to hear you—because they think you can either help them, entertain them, or inform them. At the least, they want to know you identify with their feelings, attitudes, or values. Therefore, you must establish credibility with them immediately. Why should they listen to you? How are you similar (or different) from them? Why are you qualified to talk on the subject?

Third, the opening sets the overall direction of the situation and lets the audience know what's about to happen. This control puts them at ease and gives them a reason to listen.

To arouse interest. To establish rapport and credibility. To give direction. With these purposes for an opening in mind, you can start with an opening to your topic or with an "opening to the opening."

In an "opening to the opening," you can do the following.

React to another's introduction of you: "I appreciate your comments about my cycle trip—that should keep me humble during this next ten minutes." (It lets the audience identify with your embarrassment.)

Disclose something about yourself: "Since Bill brought up college alma maters in his earlier remarks, I bet you didn't know that I was pictured in my senior album on the "Most Likely To . . ." page—Most Likely to Have More Clothes Than I Could Afford to Send to the Cleaners. Have you ever been stupid enough to take all your white shirts to the cleaners on the same day? And unlucky enough to have them disappear into a black hole in their back room? Well, guess what. This morning. . . ." (Sharing your disaster makes you human and vulnerable, so the audience can identify with you.)

Comment on the special occasion: "I congratulate you on this silver anniversary of your medical service to the community." Or, "I'm happy to share with you the thrill of dedicating your new church building." (A warm fuzzy will inspire the audience.)

Remember a special date or cause: "On this anniversary date of the traffic accident where so many of our colleagues lost their lives, I want to go on record as one who remembers their sacrifice." Or, "This month marks the anniversary of the two-year partnership between our companies. We've seen changes in...." (A common, shared experience with the audience evokes positive feelings.)

Compliment the audience: "Many of you have set aside these two days for the meeting at great expense to your own work schedules; you have put caring above your sales commissions." Or, "I understand that your organization has won four awards for distinguished achievement in publishing." Or, "Thank you for being so considerate in asking me to join you for the weekend golf tournament." (All of these provide warm fuzzies for the audience.)

Respond to the audience's attitude: "I know that I'm not addressing an unbiased group on this subject, and I appreciate your willingness to hear my views." Or, "I realize that some of you may have had several other urgent things on your agenda this afternoon until your supervisor changed the game plan and asked that you attend this presentation. But I can assure you that the issue is an important one to your future here." (Such comments pique their interest and show honesty in your approach and understanding of their viewpoint or plight.)

Refer to something prior in the program: "As George told his shaggy-dog story earlier, I recalled my own similar frustrations with such management attitudes." Or, "I understand that your meeting programs for the past four months have centered around.... I want to continue that emphasis with a new perspective." (These reflections show an interest in their organization and shared earlier experience.)

Tell about your arrival: "You may think it's easy to drive downtown from the suburbs at 5:00 a.m. Well, this morning had to set some kind of record." (Mentioning that you are susceptible to the same problems they are makes you seem human and often adds humor.)

Reflect on why you were selected for the presentation: "I'm not quite sure why Martha asked me to present these ideas when so many of you are equally qualified to. Perhaps she wanted a parent's view of the whole issue without regard to the economics that charge the decision-making atmosphere." Or, "I'm no Bible scholar—as you'll soon see—so I definitely can't quote chapter and verse on my ideas. But I do think I'm probably an expert when it comes to one who has been repeatedly forgiven." (This opening statement piques their curiosity and shows your understanding of the situation.)

Recognize key people in the audience: "Before I begin, I want to thank Vice President Jordan Moore for being here tonight to lend his support to this special cause. It has been his active involvement that has opened the channels we have needed to organize this movement throughout the local business community." (Such comments show admiration and identification with the audience's point of view.)

Express your pleasure at being the presenter: "I want you to know how much I've looked forward to addressing your group tonight. Many of you are old friends who've made me look very good through the years." (Expressing your eagerness to be with them compliments the audience and lets them know you're prepared.)

With any of the openings to the opening, keep the remarks brief—no more than two or three sentences—before you move on to the real introduction to your topic.

☞ **29. The Opening**

Once you have established rapport, immediately let your audience know that it is to their benefit to hear what you have to say. If you're tempted to drone on and on with preliminaries, keep in the back of your mind that your audience is always asking, "What's in it for me? Should I tune out? Tiptoe out for coffee? Catch Mary Smith before she leaves for the day?"

Again, you have several choices to arouse interest in your topic.

Ask a rhetorical question: "Is it possible to never feel depressed again—for any reason?" Or, "Can we improve our health-care benefits to employees for less money than we're now paying? I'd like to present some figures."

Make a startling statement: "One out of four girls between the ages of ten and nineteen will be assaulted sometime in her teen years."

Quote an authority: "The Apostle Paul had confidence in his source of love: 'For I am persuaded that neither death nor life, nor angels nor principalities ... nor any other created thing, shall be able to separate us from the love of God which is in Jesus Christ our Lord'" (Rom. 8:38).

Challenge the audience: "I dare you to leave tonight unchanged in your attitude about the poverty in our community." Or, "I challenge you to set a quota for your sales territory that will motivate even your best performer."

Declare your purpose: "My purpose is simply to confront you with both sides of the political issue." Or, "After you see our designs, I want your approval on the funding we need to begin construction immediately."

Brief your audience: "I have three points to make tonight: Our school-age population has increased 48 percent this past thirteen months. We do not have adequate school facilities. And we are going to have to decide between a tax increase and an inadequate education for our children that will eventually cost us millions of dollars in welfare, crime, and lost wages."

Illustrate an attitude or create a mood: "With the kind of service our support center provides, making a sales call is like walking across a field of firecrackers with a match in your back pocket. Yesterday, a customer I had promised delivery to by August 1 grabbed me by the lapel and threatened a lawsuit. In Atlanta, it's no better...."

Present a startling statistic: "We have spent over $465,000 in the last three months on overseas shipping charges."

Mention a current event: "This morning's news bombarded us with stories of the plight of Houston flood victims. Yet despite this latest disaster, we have yet to convince the majority of our population of the need for appropriate insurance of all kinds—flood, health, disability."

Share common ground with your audience: "How many of you have eaten in a fast-food restaurant at least three times in the last week?" Look around at the raised hands. Or, "Let me tell you about the kitchen conditions where I ate breakfast this morning and you tell me if you and I don't need to push for tighter inspection standards."

Use a visual aid: "Look at this necklace against the black velvet. What does this sparkle have to do with mining conditions in Wyoming? I want to point out three things that make this diamond undesirable to our buyers."

Define a term: "GNC is a term you've seen in the company newsletter for about four issues now. GNC. The Get-Next Command. You think we're talking about computers. No, this term refers to...."

Compare or contrast two things: "Men look at garage shelving and say, 'How functional!' Women look at garage shelving and say, 'How ugly!'"

Explain the significance of your topic: "At the conclusion of this field trip, our dietitians will have gathered enough nutritional knowledge to protect Americans from four dreaded diseases."

Promise advantages such as peace of mind, money, self-satisfaction, accomplishment, faith, love, approval, success: "At the conclusion of this presentation you will have at your disposal three techniques to increase your income through your part-time hobby."

All these methods can help you establish credibility and arouse interest. Several such well-known introductions are found in the Bible. Paul's address at Mars Hill began: "Men of Athens, I perceive that in all things you are very religious" (Acts 17:22). Scholars interpret his meaning in several ways. To some, it is a provocative, challenging statement. According to other interpretations, his opening was a compliment and a shared experience with the audience—their interest in the supernatural.

Barnabas, in his introduction of Paul to the disciples, began with a briefing of the facts surrounding Paul's conversion (Acts 9:27). In other words, Barnabas began with a "You can't imagine what just happened to Paul on his way to Damascus. Just listen to this. . . ."

Philip, in talking to the Ethiopian eunuch, began with the question, "Do you understand what you are reading?" (Acts 8:30) as he climbed up into the chariot and led him to faith. His question forced an answer and smoothly led his listener to the real point of personal faith.

Select your opening according to your purpose, the occasion and audience, and your topic. In fact, you may use the preceding list to work out several possible openings before making a final decision.

Before we leave the topic of openings, here are a few don'ts:

Don't routinely begin with a joke. Few humorous openings really work because often the humor has nothing at all to do with the topic and merely leaves the audience hanging as to its relevance. It's like having someone rush up to you in the grocery store with a broad smile and arms extended and then slink away sheepishly without a word when she realizes she's mistaken you for someone else.

Even a funny story that relates to your subject usually works better a little later in the presentation because at the beginning the audience is still deciding how to react to you as a person.

Don't promise something that you can't deliver. You should never present benefits that are impossible to attain. If you promise to tell an audience a sure way to lose fifteen pounds in two weeks and then tell them nothing they haven't already tried, they're going to feel disappointed. If you promise the boss three ways to reduce shipping costs, and none of them turns out to be practical in your office environment, the boss will walk away thinking you are out of touch with reality.

Finally, don't start with negatives. Don't apologize that you're unprepared. Don't complain about the room setup. Don't denigrate the city. Don't offend with bad language or prejudicial statements.

To sum up: An opening should arouse interest and establish rapport and credibility with your audience. You have a variety of ways to do one or both. The following should illustrate the big difference an appropriate opening makes:

Uh, I don't know why I'm up here, but I guess it was my unlucky day or something. Anyway, I think I'm supposed to be giving you an update on the Monroe survey. Shipping costs. I've got my notes somewhere. The gist of our findings is that we're wasting a lot of money at that plant site. And we've got a few suggestions for making some changes.

Versus:

Would anyone like to take a guess at how much money we spent on express shipping services during last quarter? It was $23,000 in our Monroe office alone! We've just completed a survey conducted by an independent auditing firm and found that 85 percent of that cost was waste—shipping charges that could have been avoided if we had properly scheduled to meet our manufacturing deadlines. As a result of that study, we have three recommendations that could reduce that expenditure to less than $3,000 within the next thirty days.

☞ **30. The Body**

Organize everything around your central message—that one- or two-sentence statement that you decided on as a road map at the beginning of your preparation. Most presentations will fall into one of four categories:

- To inform
- To persuade
- To inspire/praise
- To entertain

To Inform:
Absenteeism cost our company $2,000,000 last year, and we predict a 30 percent increase in the new year.

To Persuade:
Absenteeism costs our company too much; therefore, I'm proposing that we begin health-awareness programs that reduce stress, prevent disease, and increase overall fitness because healthier employees miss less work and are more productive.

To Inspire/Praise:
Our average employee misses fewer than 1.2 days per year for health-related reasons. We commend you for your progressive attitude about proper nutrition, exercise,

and overall fitness. We plan to offer a $500 bonus to any employee who has a perfect attendance record for the year.

To Entertain:
To maintain your health, when you're basically a lazy person, can be time consuming. It took me a week to map out a jogging trail along my driveway. In fact, a friend of mine the other day said it took him four days to get his cycle greased because. . . .

You may again decide to fine tune your overview message to fit one of these categories. You then select your supporting facts, reasons, or illustrations. For example, look at the following possibilities.

To inform: Key message
    Fact #1
    Fact #2
    Fact #3
To persuade: Key message/action wanted
    Reason #1
    Reason #2
    Reason #3
To inspire/praise: Key message
    Illustration or fact #1
    Illustration or fact #2
    Illustration or fact #3
To entertain: Key point
    Anecdote or illustration #1
    Anecdote or illustration #2
    Anecdote or illustration #3

◗ Variations for Developing the Basic Framework
Within these basic structures, your topic may lead to some variations such as the following arrangements:
Topical: "We recommend a combination of ways to

stay healthy—nutrition, exercise, stress reduction, no substance abuse."

Most important to least important: "The most important way is avoidance of drugs/alcohol. The second most important is eating properly. The third most important is proper exercise."

Problem to solution: "Absenteeism is costing us two million dollars annually. Most absences are health-related. We need to teach our employees how to stay healthy and reinforce their efforts through company-sponsored exercise facilities, subsidized meal plans, and substance-abuse counseling."

Chronological: "In 1970 absenteeism cost us $X. In 1980 it cost $X. This coming year we predict a 15-percent increase totaling $X unless we take immediate action. I suggest a company-sponsored health-maintenance plan be implemented during the next three years. In the first and second quarters of 1992, we could provide. . . . In the second half of the year, we. . . ."

Comparison/contrast: "Our absenteeism rate is twice as high as the industry average. Yet astoundingly, our average employee is younger, lives closer to the job, works shorter hours. . . ."

Geographical: "Our absenteeism rate in Atlanta is . . . because. . . . In Dallas, it's . . . because. . . . In Minneapolis, the rate is . . . because. . . ."

Spatial/physical form: "In the north wing, we could accommodate an indoor track. In the south wing, we could set up a small cafeteria. . . ."

Cause to effect/effect to cause: "Employees often work twelve-hour days and do not have time to exercise after they return to their homes. Therefore, they do not take time to prepare nutritional meals or to exercise. . . . Our average employee asks for a transfer every six months due to on-the-job stress. We think this stress is related to short deadlines, improperly working equipment. . . ."

Frequency: "The most commonly reported absence is

due to respiratory infections. The second most commonly reported illness is stomach flu. . . ."

Most difficult to least difficult: "Our biggest challenge will be to pay for the health facilities. Our next biggest challenge will be to find qualified medical advisers. . . ."

Objections/answers: "Our biggest objection from management will be the cost. However, studies in companies similar to ours show that health prevention costs much less than absenteeism. . . ."

Goal/steps: "Our number-one goal is to have an average of no more than one absence per employee annually by the end of 1996. Here are the three steps necessary to. . . ."

Status quo/change: "We now give all employees ten days sick leave each year. Under this new plan, we would provide only five days of sick leave, but would offer a bonus of $X per day of unused leave."

Feature/benefits: "This exercise bike has a tilt bar that. . . . This feature allows the rider to change positions and exercise different abdominal muscles simply by. . . ."

Procedures: "The first step is to appoint a management committee. . . . The second step is to form a volunteer employee advisory board. . . ."

Narration: "One of our managers, John Jones, noted the number of sick days after stress-filled weeks in the Leola plant. Some of his people reported. . . ."

Description: "The food service would include. . . . The exercise room will have four rowing machines, each designed to. . . ."

Your presentation may encompass one or several different frameworks. For example, your main framework may be problem-to-solution. But under your point about proper nutrition, you may mention features of the food facility you want to fund.

My purpose in providing such an extensive list is to generate a number of ways for you to think about your topic. Because once you understand the wide variety of ways available to arrange supporting detail, you'll probably generate many more ideas than you'll have time to present.

Then with your overview statement (road map) and your key points shuffled into some overall framework, look for anecdotes, statistics, explanations, testimonials, facts, or illustrations to "flesh out" or further support your points.

☞ 31. Persuasive Strategies

Before we go further in the organizing or planning process, let's take time out to consider specifically persuasive presentations.

▶ Strategy #1: Message Upfront
Give your recommendation/desired action up front.

Most people consider persuasive presentations to a boss or client to be the most difficult of all because so much is at stake in the audience's action or inaction. Therefore, presenters fall into the common trap of "laying the groundwork" before getting to the key action or attitude they want from listeners. Some presenters fear that giving a key recommendation or statement of the desired action up front is too strong.

In the business setting, decision-makers become restless with the delayed approach. They wonder what you're leading up to and why you're being cagey. Even in other settings, the once-upon-a-time approach makes audiences begin to squirm. They want the *TV Guide's* storyline before they decide to stay tuned. In fact, buyers frequently interrupt sellers with a lengthy lead-in: "Excuse me, but exactly what is it you're selling?" Don't make your own audience listen in the dark.

Generally, knowing the punchline up front comforts the audience and helps them understand your supporting details without suspense.

‣ **Strategy #2: Read Between the Lines**
Decide if you want to refute the other side of an argument or merely to support your own. You may unnecessarily anger an audience with the opposing viewpoint if you are continually focusing on the stupidity of their reasoning. You may have more success if you simply build your own case and let them come to realize their fallacy.

‣ **Strategy #3: Just the Facts**
Use fair and objective language, not overblown exaggerations and vague, unsupported claims. "Ninety percent of our orders in 1989 were from repeat buyers" is much more factual and persuasive than "Belco can meet all your computer needs."

‣ **Strategy #4: Positive/Negative Appeal**
Determine whether to use a positive or a negative appeal: "You will live longer and feel better if you exercise," versus "If you don't exercise, your chances of heart disease are increased by. . . ."

‣ **Strategy #5: A One-Track Approach**
Avoid a hedging, wishy-washy approach in such statements as: "I didn't look up the exact figures, but. . . ."; "I'm not completely up to date on this, but. . ."; "Well, I know there are always two sides to this issue, and you probably can find some holes in this, but. . . ."; "I understand where the Marketing people are coming from and they have a point. But my point is. . . ."

Your audience probably knows all the sides and points. Generally, the best strategy is to focus on yours—factually and with adequate preparation.

☞ **32. Transitions**

Once you've decided on the framework for your key points, be sure to tie them together. Transitions carry your listener from point A to B. Each new point should begin with an overview statement and conclude with a bridging statement to lead the audience to the next key point.

Example:
(Overview) "...Not only is stress reduction important to good health, but so is proper nutrition." *(Bridge)* "So you can see how eating right can reduce heart disease and risks for cancer...."

Example:

(Bridge) "You may be thinking that all those preventative measures sound good. But where will you find the time?" *(Overview)* "Well, we have decided on three ways to help you stay healthy without lengthening your work day. The first is our intent to open a jogging track...." *(Bridge)* "...So the jogging track should be open by the end of the year. In the meantime, a bigger concern you may have is...."

In addition to these transition words, there are several other ways to signal your audience that you're ready to move to the next idea: a summary of your points to this juncture in your presentation; a long pause; a change of locations or positions to deliver your next point; a new visual. Whichever method you use, just be sure to take your listeners with you as you move from thought to thought.

Smooth transitions increase listener retention and exemplify a polished, prepared presentation. Transitions are to a speech what paragraphs are to a letter.

☞ **33. Closings**

"And in closing..." makes our ears perk up as listeners, but you as a speaker want more. You want retention of what you've said and often you want action from your audience.

If you are presenting simply to inform, your closing may be only a summary of your key points. If your purpose is to persuade—to change an opinion, to make a decision, to approve a purchase, to support a cause, to encourage participation—you will call for the specific next action: To enclose a check, to approve the transfer, to fill out the order form, to volunteer to give blood. The action may be immediate or delayed.

If you are presenting to inspire or praise, you will want to end with a summary of your commendation and your expectations for the future. The basic idea here is to move people to action or to a state of mind by touching their emotions. Often you will close this kind of presentation with an emotional anecdote, a fiery quote, or a prediction for future commitment and success.

> A speech is like a love affair—any fool can start one, but it requires considerable skill to end one.
>
> —E.C. McKenzie

You may announce your closing with a statement such as: "To wrap up our discussion"; "One final thought"; "As I conclude, I want to relate one last story about. . ."; "Let me leave you with this idea"; "I'll end with two challenges"; "To put it succinctly, we must. . . ."

When your audience hears these words, they perk up because you're going to give order to all they've heard. You're going to make it all worthwhile by wrapping their thinking in a nice neat package ready for delivery and action.

Think of your speech as a loop; the end must tie back

to the beginning. If you open with a provocative question, answer it at the closing. If you startle them with statistics at the opening, tell them how they can change the statistics. If you begin with an anecdote, remind them of how the anecdote could have turned out differently. If you start out with a challenge, leave them with the first step in meeting that challenge. If you promise to inform, simply tell them what you told them.

We seek to dominate no other nation. We ask no territorial expansion. We oppose imperialism. We desire reduction in world armaments. We believe in democracy; we believe in freedom; we believe in peace. We offer to every nation of the world the handclasp of the good neighbor. Let those who wish our friendship look us in the eye and take our hand.
                    —Franklin D. Roosevelt, speaking
                              on international affairs

A strong closing summarizes simply but dramatically.

Whatever technique you choose, end with a wallop rather than a whimper. Avoid rumblings and mumblings such as: "I guess that's all I've got to say"; "I think I'm about through unless you have questions"; "That's all they asked me to say"; "I'm sorry I couldn't get the overhead to work, but I hope you got the idea of how the shuttle will look"; "Oh, one thing I forgot to say earlier is that. . . ."; "Oh, you all look too serious—lighten up. This is only a job."

In closing, don't apologize, be long-winded, bring up new points, throw in irrelevant details, change the mood of the group, or shuffle off with no closing at all.

Instead, pack a wallop. Reinforce your talk with a summary statement, make an appeal, look ahead to the future, ask a rhetorical question, tell an anecdote, quote some higher authority on the issue, or use a related bit of humor.

If you intend to have a question-answer period (discussed in part 6), do so before you deliver your closing remarks. Your close should be the last memory on your listener's mind.

☞ 34. The Finishing Touches

You have an opening, a body, transitions, and a closing. You're almost there, but this last step is the difference between a mediocre, adequate presentation and one that has impact. Shuffle your outline or full script before you and see where you can polish it to perfection with these additions.

▶ Audience-Involvement Techniques

Involve your audience with techniques such as questions, opinion "polls," demonstrations, mention of names of those in the group, requests for them to move physically. "How many of you here have visited our headquarters office since last January?" gets the audience to respond with a lifted hand. "How many of you prefer hot weather to cold—let me see your hands," means each listener has to tune in long enough for you to interpret the information you receive.

Questions such as "What would you do if. . ." or "Has this ever happened to you?" make an audience think with you, even if they don't have to respond overtly.

"Turn to the person to your left and give a thirty-second description of your part in the project" adds variety and a personal touch to your own overview.

"Can anyone give me an example of this principle of

ethics at work in a community church?" customizes your point to a particular audience.

Audiences even like to participate vicariously through volunteers from the group or demonstrations with an object or procedure. "I know each division has one person who probably stands out as a mentor—Joan Gandee is one such person" tends to make the group glance at Joan and think for themselves. "Would all of you turn your chairs to face the screen at the back of the room" provides a change-of-pace activity to the monotony of the spoken word from a fixed angle.

Just keep in mind that audience participation works best when everyone feels at ease and has a choice. Pressure to participate—even to lift a hand in response to a question—may intimidate a few. Be your own cheerleader, and don't ask the audience to do anything you wouldn't do. An enthusiastic demeanor helps.

Such participation always makes the information seem fresh and customized to your audience.

◗ Anecdotes

Particularly effective anecdotes are those the audience can most identify with—those based on their common feelings, predicaments, dilemmas, decisions. Mine your own experience, those experiences of "average" people you know, or experiences of the famous as related in their biographies or TV comments. Anecdotes make dry points memorable.

◗ Analogies

Analogies also improve clarity and retention. The more complex the idea, the more important it is to simplify and illustrate by comparison. Analogies can even provide a consistent framework throughout a section of your presentation. For example, think how many times you've heard the human eye and all its parts compared to a camera, this is an excellent analogy for clarifying.

We need to look no farther than Scripture. Probably the best known analogies are biblical parables: Concern over the unrepentant means leaving the ninety-nine sheep to look for the lost one. Joy over the repentant compares to that of the father when his prodigal son returns from the "far country." Such visual and emotional analogies help audiences see and feel. The Master Storyteller obviously appealed to the common man and woman with universal insights and emotions.

◗ Quotes

Quotes add impact because they defer to an authority higher than your own as presenter. Quotations that find their way into print are usually succinctly and colorfully worded, crystallizing the key idea better than you can yourself.

As you prepare, check references that categorize quotes by subject to find just the touch of awe—or humor—you need. And if you really want to add credibility with your quote, hold the actual *Wall Street Journal* clipping up during your presentation and read from it. This is authenticity at its best.

◗ Humor

Humor grabs attention the way no other technique quite can. And humor encompasses much more than merely telling a joke. It may be a light approach to a point, a witty offhanded comment, or a self-deprecating story. Your purpose isn't to bring down the house with wildly funny stories; the audience doesn't expect Johnny Carson. Just a light approach at making your point is sufficient and memorable.

Never use unrelated humor because it sounds contrived and disjointed, distracting your listeners from your point rather than reinforcing it.

Simply make the point. Tell the funny story. Restate the point.

Thank you for your attention. Some of you are obviously into assertive listening.
> —*Rich's Current Humor Newsletter.*
> July, 1989

Our After Dinner keynoter comes to us from a humble beginning. He started out as an After Snack speaker.
> —*Rich's Current Humor Newsletter*
> July, 1989

If you can't remember a joke—don't dis-member it.
> —E.C. McKenzie

Most of the speakers you'll hear today consti-tute a sort of who's who in the industry. I'm more in the category of who's he.
> —Michael Iapoce

Remember that timing is everything with humor. One word botched, mumbled, or out of order can sink the ship. Practice your delivery.

The humorous points may be the only part of your pre-sentation your audience remembers. That fact has slapped me in the face several times over the years. In my writing workshops for corporate clients, I make a point that unnecessary tense and mood changes can alter the meaning of a sentence. To reinforce that point, I show a two-minute video vignette about such confusion and then warn students about airplane pilots who announce: "We would like to thank you for flying So-and-So Airlines today." Two years after a particular workshop, my path again crossed with an attendee. He commented on the value of the course and assured me he remembered the airline joke. Now, I'll have to admit the humorous touches on that point are outstanding. But to my chagrin, the joke illustrated the least important concept of the entire course! Humor has power.

Another story I use creates audience identification: about the 6:00 A.M. breakfast for which I arrived so tired and flustered that, without realizing it, I brushed my teeth and put on my makeup in the men's restroom.

A willingness to share personal experiences and tell stories on yourself provides an excellent source of original humor that everyone can dig up from the past. Audiences appreciate the candor in using your own weaknesses or misery to make a point. Just be careful that the stories aren't boastful rather than humorous.

And remember that the longer the story, the funnier it needs to be. Attention spans are short for a single point. Lengthy stories can end in disappointment at the punchline. Avoid warning your audience "Here comes a joke" with those lead-ins like "That reminds me of the story about. . . ." Just get into the story and make it appear spontaneous.

Always know enough about your audience that you can slant your humorous story to them, their point of view, and their mood.

As with quotes, editors and writers have made the speaker's job much easier by collecting and categorizing humorous stories under easily accessible headings. Here are several books that I recommend: *A Funny Thing Happened on the Way to the Boardroom* by Michael Iapoce; *Speaker's and Toastmaster's Handbook* by Herbert V.

Prochnow; *14,000 Quips & Quotes for Writers & Speakers* by E.C. McKenzie.

▶ Colorful Phrasing

Metaphors, similes, alliteration (repetition of sounds), and repetition of words or structures add the polish of a professional. Representative John LaFalce writing in *INC* magazine (July 1989) used an apt analogy in his line: "Some say Section 89 is like throwing an atom bomb at an anthill—and missing the anthill." This is the type of image that can make or break a presentation. Jesus, the Master Communicator, also exemplified such colorful use of language in His comments to His disciples: "Feed My sheep" (John 21:17), and "Follow Me and I will make you fishers of men" (Matt. 4:19). Simple, but powerful.

Your initial attempts will usually be bread-and-butter expressions. But as you practice your presentation, you can always substitute more colorful, memorable phrasing to make your points.

Don't neglect these finishing touches; they can breathe life into your ideas.

Rehearsing Your Presentation

Once you have a stack of notes in your hands or a full outline and draft of a presentation, you'll feel much better about the whole business of presenting a new budget to your boss or a new product line to your customer. Words in black and white are reassuring and promising. But you're not ready to deliver your ideas yet. Editing comes next.

If you don't edit yourself *before* you speak, your listeners will do it *as* you speak. If you seem to be hurried or off schedule and in danger of not finishing on time, they'll keep one eye on their watches and the other on your stack of notes. Their anxiety will grow.

So to put your audience at ease, clearly let them know you're in control of your information—not the other way around. Practice and timing are essential to that control. Despite your attention to timing from the very beginning of your preparation, you'll need your practice session as the last check.

☞ 35. Timing—Where and How to Add or Cut

If you've kept in mind the "one page equals two minutes" rule as you have prepared, you probably have the total length about right. But you must give one more consideration to it: Timing should indicate emphasis. Have you spent only thirty seconds on a major reason to spend $10,000, and seven minutes on an anecdote in the introduction? If so, now is the time to reshuffle your information so that timing corresponds to the importance of the ideas.

To emphasize a key idea, elaborate. Add facts, statistics, quotes, anecdotes or other details. To lengthen the entire presentation, come up with additional key points. Don't simply try to add more words to the points already well made.

On the other hand, you may discover that you need to cut some information. Always keep in mind the audience's interest. Think of your presentation as a road map. If your audience wants to take only the interstate highways to get to their decision/destination, don't draw in all the farm-to-market roads along the way. That merely clutters the road map.

> The secret of being a bore is to tell everything.
>
> —Voltaire

> On information overload: Remember, most houseplants in the U.S. are killed by overwatering.
>
> —R. John Brockmann

When your presentation runs too long, you'll be tempted to cut the flesh and leave the skeleton. That is, you'll want to retain all your key points and omit the stories, quotes, visuals. Don't. Remember that these tidbits help make your key points memorable.

Sometimes you may be able to condense your presentation without leaving out anything of substance by simply improving sloppy wording. If you've written a draft, keep the language tight. Note how succinct the quotes included in this book are. They convey ideas in nouns and verbs. Adjectives and adverbs clutter; for a stronger impact, retain only the meat of the idea.

If you are writing a script either to read or to practice in extemporaneous speaking, remember that one page (about 250 words) is about two minutes of spoken delivery. To be accurate, read and time your presentation several times. Keep in mind that you tend to present your talk more quickly in rehearsal than in real life. So always leave yourself a safety net. Count on the fact that a written presentation will take longer to deliver with ad libs, visuals, audience reaction, and extemporaneous comments that the audience evokes.

As you practice, record on your notes or outline the timing of each portion of your presentation. For example, if a certain anecdote takes three minutes, jot that on your outline. These notations help you make spur-of-the-moment decisions about what to eliminate or to add if you run long or short during the actual presentation. Distractions, late starts, questions, and other interruptions may force you to do some on-the-spot adjustments to end on time.

But timing is not your sole consideration in the editing phase. There are other items that may need attention.

Weed out generalities, clichés, and platitudes. Make your points specific and support them with facts. Substitute your own fresh wording for clichés. Plus, platitudes give audiences time to doze.

Use statistics with care. First of all, they should be up to date. Nothing will destroy credibility like having numbers that are ten years old. Also, make sure your statistics aren't misleading. If your competitor's profit increased by 400 percent last year, that may mean that he sold four quilts rather than one. "Averages" are often deceptive. You can describe a hiker crossing a desert at 125 degrees and then plunging into a mountain stream at 41 degrees, and conclude that the temperature on his vacation averaged a pleasant 83 degrees.

Be wary of using too many statistics and round off the ones you select. Bombarding your listeners with numbers confuses them so that they recall none. To make those you select meaningful, bring them within the understanding of your audience.

For example, a headline from the Scripps Howard News Service reads: "Taxes cost 163 minutes for every eight working hours." That puts the "high cost of taxes" in perspective; we work almost three hours out of eight to pay them. Then the writer goes on to illustrate the other facts: Food and tobacco cost 59 minutes; transportation, 40 minutes; medical care, 39 minutes; clothing, 24 minutes; recreation, 20 minutes; and all other expenses, 50 minutes.

Finally, be sure to source information borrowed from others—that adds credibility. We have become wary of the political reporter's "unidentified sources claim that. . ." line.

Just remember that it's easier to gather statistics and facts than to make them interesting and memorable. Don't get sidetracked on the first and omit the second.

☞ 36. To Write or Not to Write a Complete Script?

Reading from a full script, speaking from an outline or notes, or memorizing—these are your delivery choices until technology makes it possible and affordable for all of us to have a portable teleprompter the size of our pocket calculator.

Let's discuss the pros and cons of each method.

◗ Reading from a Full Script
Here are the pros:

● A script quiets your fears that you will go blank. Every single word in black and white in front of you provides a security blanket.

● Your timing will be perfect. You know exactly how long each point takes, and with practice in reading, you know that you can end on time.

● Your language will be more exact, precise, colorful, and grammatically correct than if you speak extemporaneously. You'll have opportunity to rework and polish each sentence.

● You will have something "official" to give to the media if you're a spokesperson for your organization. Scripts are often necessary if you have to gain official approval of your exact wording from your company's public affairs officer or if you are otherwise concerned that you will be misquoted. You can, however, always provide a written text to the media for their quotes and still deliver the thoughts extemporaneously.

> Politicians have four speeches for each occasion: what they have written down, what they actually say, what they wish they had said, and what they are quoted as saying the next day.
>
> —E.C. McKenzie

And now for the cons:

● You'll have little eye contact with your audience. No matter how much you've practiced your upward glances, you'll be tempted to read more and more. Particularly in the all-important beginning when you either win or lose your audience's attention. The reciprocity of the situation is lost. When you speak to an

audience eye to eye, you have their attention because they have yours. When you stare at the script, their temptation is to reciprocate by looking at their own notes or glancing around the room at others' reactions.
• Your words lose their genuineness and intimacy. When you can't look your audience in the face, you lose one of your best techniques for credibility. The effect is the same as when a lover who speaks a language different from his sweetheart pulls a scrap of paper from his back pocket and reads, "I love you for your beautiful personality, your thoughtfulness, and your sensitivity." She gazes at his eyes while he gazes at the paper.
• You won't sound natural. Even with the skill of an experienced lecturer, you'll have difficulty not sounding stilted—much like the "average Joe" testimonials on TV commercials.
• Your gestures will be nonexistent or contrived. To be effective, gestures should come from the gut. Reading stifles that unconscious signal to gesture where necessary.
• You will be tied to a podium or table to deliver your presentation, without the freedom to move toward visuals or your audience.
• You may lose your place. The danger is that you will frantically find yourself paused in an inappropriate spot groping for the next phrase or idea.
• The audience may wonder if the words and ideas are really yours. Did you have a ghostwriter friend or colleague help you? If so, should you really receive the credit for any impact the presentation might have?
• If it's an audience you know well, they'll contrast the way you usually talk and gesture with this different image and focus on the disparity between the two.

As you can see, the advantages of reading from a script can be achieved with almost any other method if you prepare adequately. The cons can rarely be overcome. Only on a rare occasion should you ever read from a script.

But if you decide, against all advice from the experts, to do so anyway, here are some tips to make you more effective:

● Dictate the text in one sitting. The process will be faster and the tone will be more informal and appropriate. After you have a draft you can polish.

● Prepare your script for reading by marking it. Double or triple space the text. Skip extra lines between paragraphs to signal yourself that you're finished with an idea. Mark a single / to indicate a pause; mark a double // to indicate a longer pause. With a highlighting pen, mark key words and phrases that need special emphasis. Choose certain colors to help you quickly grasp the layout of your ideas.

For example, use green for basic key points, red for examples and statistics, blue for the introduction to a long anecdote. Leave pages unstapled so that you can lay them aside more easily as you read each one. Type in both uppercase and lowercase. All uppercase lines are much more difficult to read. Don't break a sentence, paragraph, or list between two pages. Insert margin notes for use of visuals, demonstrations, or other movements away from the lectern.

Always, always, always deliver your speech from the same copy you used to practice rather than from a new copy with a different layout. Your mind will "photograph" chunks and the first words of a paragraph will help your brain recall the remainder.

● Check the lighting at the lectern or table beforehand to make sure you can see your script.

● Don't try to hide your script. The audience will know you're reading, and trying to discreetly hide the script looks deceptive and silly.

● Be aware that you will probably read too quickly and

will need to make a conscious effort to slow down.
● Concentrate on the meaning of what you're saying rather than the phrasing. With concentration, your inflection, pauses, and gestures will improve.

A new pastor stopped a respected member of the congregation on her way out of the church door on Sunday morning:

"Well, Mrs. Jones, how did you like the sermon?"

"Not bad. Not bad."

Not quite pleased with that backhanded compliment, he persisted, "So did you see anything particularly wrong with it?"

"Well, now that you mention it, Pastor, I guess I do have three observations: First, you read it. Second, you didn't read it well. And third, it wasn't worth reading."

— story commonly circulated among speakers

◗ Speaking from Notes or Outline

By far, this is the most effective delivery method for the majority of presenters. Following are the pros and cons for your own evaluation.

Pros:
● You can maintain the all-important eye contact throughout.
● Your ideas will seem genuine and intimate because they will be spoken in your own spontaneous way with fresh inflection and emotion.
● Your gestures will be natural.
● Notes will provide you with an outline for security but freedom to move around in front of the group to use visuals or to interact with the audience.

● You will have no fear to add or delete ideas, facts, or illustrations as necessary to suit audience needs or reactions. You'll eliminate the fear of losing your place and your poise or of trying to find a spot in the script to jump back in.

Cons:
● Your exact phrasing will not be as precise as when read from a polished script.
● Your timing will vary.

If you agree that this method lends the advantages you need, prepare two kinds of delivery aids: a practice outline and a delivery outline.

A practice outline is a detailed outline on multiple pages. Again, the benefit of such detail is a memory crutch for practice. But the negatives are that you will fumble with the pages during delivery and refer to the outline too frequently, losing eye contact and destroying credibility.

For your actual delivery, construct only an outline of key words that will trigger your memory with just a glance.

The Idea Wheel
Another variant of this single-view outline is the idea wheel illustrated in Figure 1 on page 103.

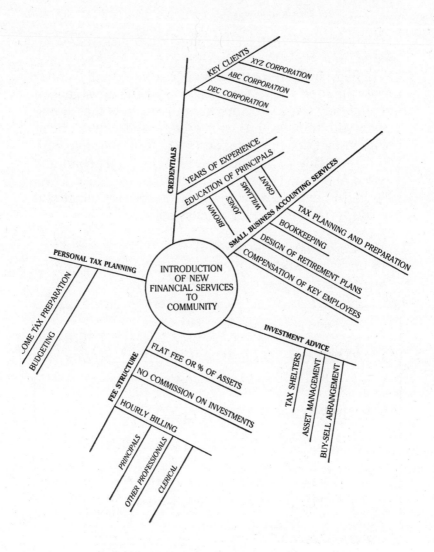

Figure 1: The idea wheel is a thinking tool that also becomes a speaking outline

This idea wheel lets you capture several hours' worth of ideas in a single view. You can easily use this outline to give a ten-minute talk on a school fundraiser or a half-day presentation on your financial services. The advantage in keeping the whole structure in front of you is that in one glance you know where you've been and where you're going. In fact, for presentations in small-group meetings, you may decide to put the idea wheel on a flipchart and let your audience follow the structure of your talk. It will help them keep questions and comments on target and provide a memory aid for discussion.

The Card Half-&-Half Script
The card method combines a full script with key topics as memory joggers. See Figure 2 below.

---

3 MIN.
TRANSITION: SO HOW CAN WE DIG OUR WAY OUT OF THE PAPER BLIZZARD?

3. GIVE YOUR PEOPLE A CHALLENGE.

    —SURVEY RESPONSES—28% "UNCHAL-LENGED"
    —ANECDOTE—UTILITY COMPANY
    —T.—STATISTICS FROM GARFIELD

CONCLUSION: "CLEARLY, OUR PEOPLE SHOULD BE ABLE TO VOLUNTEER FOR ADVISORY COMMITTEES."

Figure 2: The card half-&-half script provides structure and security while allowing flexibility and fresh phrasing.

With this method, you write the opening statement and the transitions for each point in polished form. Then express the meat of the idea only in key words. Those ideas will remain spontaneously fresh in the final presentation.

Here are a few other guidelines to help you handle your notes or outline during delivery:

- Always number your cards, but feel free to reshuffle them as needs change.
- Note how much time each point or illustration takes so that you can make an on-the-spot decision about what to eliminate or add if time runs short or long.
- Color code your cards (on the edges) so that you can quickly skip forward or backward if you make extemporaneous changes. Green corners for main points. Blue for subpoints or illustrations. Red for statistics.
- Memorize your opening, your closing, and your transitions between points.

No audience will mind that you use notes. After all, they want to know you're prepared. The issue is *how* you use them. To avoid depending on them too much, practice with a detailed outline. Then use only key words or phrases on an outline, note card, or idea wheel to force yourself to look at your audience.

◗ Memorizing Your Speech

The final presentation method is memorization. Again there are pros and cons.

Pros:
- If you work very hard to memorize a script verbatim with all the appropriate inflection and gestures, you will sound like a genius—although maybe a robot genius.

Cons:
- If you have a memory lapse, you will feel like an idiot and your audience will think you foolish for being so "unprepared."

If you do choose to attempt such a feat, here's how to do it:

- Prepare a written text and read it and reread it and reread it.
- Practice from the same script because your eyes will "photograph" copies of the page to aid memorization.
- Break it down into chunks and memorize one chunk at a time.
- Devise some acronym or other mnemonic device to remind you of the correct order of the chunks.
- Practice in front of a mirror to see that you retain natural facial expression and other appropriate gestures.

My suggestion is not to memorize. You'll fear going blank, particularly if there are any distractions. Memorization also makes the audience uneasy. At first they marvel and then they worry if you'll make it to the end.

☞ **37. Learning Your Material**

Read your outline, notes, or practice script over and over. Read it aloud. Time yourself on each section and record the timing in the margins. Connect the ideas in some acronym and learn to predict the next thought before your eyes catch the next prompt.

Then stand in front of a mirror to practice how often you are able to glance up from your notes.

After you've grown less dependent on your notes, memorize the opening, the transitions between key points, and the closing. That will allow you to maintain the all-important eye contact at crucial times—when you're making a first impression and your audience is deciding whether you're worth listening to, and at the conclusion when they fix in their minds how good you were.

As you practice, don't be tempted just to read through

your notes without actually expressing the key ideas in complete sentences. As someone has said, "There's no substitute for scrimmaging." The time required to express your ideas aloud in complete sentences and in the correct order will add polish and confidence to your "real" presentation. Particularly pay attention to your delivery of any funny stories. They, more than any other part of your presentation, succeed or fail based on delivery.

☞ **38. Practicing Your Delivery**

The next step is practice. Do it live, aloud, and alone. You can stand in front of a mirror, audiotape, or videotape yourself. Video is by far the best because you will be able to see distracting mannerisms, poor posture, and weak gestures. If a video is unavailable, an audiotape is the next best thing. You will catch irritating voice fillers (*aahh, uh, okay, right?*) and repetitive phrases (*Let me emphasize that...*).

Additionally, you'll become more aware of your rate of speech, the tendency to let words trail off at the end of sentences, mumbling, or poor diction. You will also note where to add emphasis and variety. Another benefit of audiotape is that once you record your presentation, you can listen and fix the material in your mind as you complete other tasks such as driving to work or eating. Tape. Listen. Rehearse again. Tape. Listen. Retape. You'll hear dramatic improvements, and, again, these improvements will build your confidence.

Finally, you can practice in front of friends, family, or colleagues and get their feedback. If they're interested, your enthusiasm and confidence will grow. If their attention wanders, you need more practice or better material.

☞ **39. Evaluating Your Feedback**

Remember that others' feedback will be biased. Your

family and friends will generally love you. Don't rely too heavily on their compliments; instead, focus on their suggestions. Neither should you ask your sharpest critic to listen to you because his or her comments may be unfairly harsh, destroying your confidence.

The following are guidelines for evaluating your practice sessions:

- Don't try to correct everything at once. Work on either slowing down your delivery or remembering your transitions. Focus on one thing at a time.
- Have a priority system for improvement. Work on learning your information first, then maybe gestures, then perhaps diction and crisp endings on words.
- Look for ideas that you stumble over. Memorize the lead-ins, transitions, and concluding points on these ideas.
- Look for flawed logic or gaps in the material that need to be revised—even at this late date. This practice is your last opportunity to make the ideas logical and clear.
- Continue to monitor your timing and remember that your actual delivery will tend to run a little longer than your practice.
- Don't be too hard on yourself. You'll always sound worse to yourself than to others. Focus on your improvements and how much your audience will benefit from hearing you.

It's really quite simple: A little editing, a little learning, a little practice, a little evaluation. Your material will become so much a part of you that the ideas will flow like water from a fountain when you bend over for a sip.

Selecting, Preparing, and Using Visuals

5

Visuals bombard us daily. Companies produce TV commercials and magazine ads to sell us their products and services. The *Wall Street Journal* gives us the economic, financial, and statistical news with symbols of oil rigs, money bags, and attaché cases. Weather forecasters predict tomorrow's conditions with a colored map. Flight attendants demonstrate proper emergency procedures for air travel. Restaurants give us photos on their menus, and their dessert carts display the real thing.

Why? Retention. Memory. Impact. Consider how the human brain works in the following situations: Do you receive most directions by street names and addresses or landmarks such as buildings and traffic signals? When friends give directions to their home, do they usually write the travel procedure in steps or draw you a map? Which do you remember better—faces or names?

Do at-home audiences more often listen to radio or watch TV? Consider music, designed to be heard. Given a choice, would audiences rather listen to a recording of their favorite artist or see him/her perform live? Do you remember the names on the movie credits as they roll

DO YOU DRAW A MAP OR WRITE TRAVEL PROCEDURES?

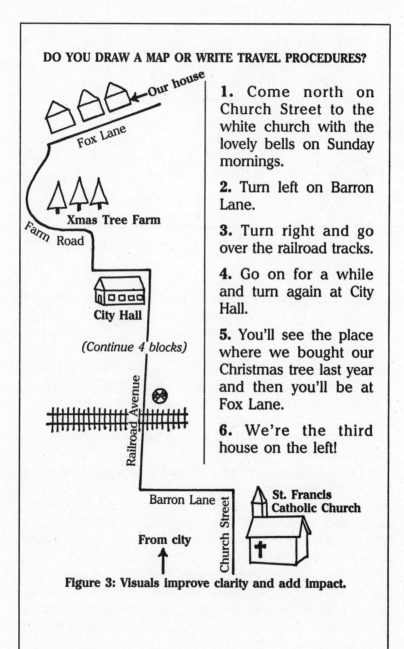

1. Come north on Church Street to the white church with the lovely bells on Sunday mornings.

2. Turn left on Barron Lane.

3. Turn right and go over the railroad tracks.

4. Go on for a while and turn again at City Hall.

5. You'll see the place where we bought our Christmas tree last year and then you'll be at Fox Lane.

6. We're the third house on the left!

Figure 3: Visuals improve clarity and add impact.

across the screen or the opening long shot of the action?

In today's environment, most audiences expect visuals. If you're giving a presentation without them, be very sure you have a *brief* message, *intriguing* content, and a *captivating* delivery style.

People learn in different ways. Some of us learn more by what we see and others learn better by what we hear. But no one would disagree that using both techniques — speaking and showing — increases retention and impact dramatically. Do you recall the hush that fell on the room where King Belshazzar and his friends saw the hand write on the wall? (Dan. 5:5) Or the effect of Jesus' referring His questioner to the inscription on Caesar's coin? (Matt. 22:20)

PEOPLE HAVE SHORT-CIRCUITING MEMORIES

Time Lapse After Presentation	*Retention*
24 hours	75%
48 hours	50%
4 days	20%

—Dorothy Leeds

University studies prove the same principles. At the University of Wisconsin, researchers determined that retention improves up to 200 percent when visual aids are used in teaching new vocabulary words. Studies at Harvard and Columbia revealed that visuals improve retention by 14 to 38 percent over presentations without visuals. Studies at the University of Pennsylvania's Wharton School of Business demonstrated that the time needed to make a point can be reduced up to 40 percent when visuals accompany an oral presentation. Additionally, this study showed that audiences rated presenters who used visuals more favorably than presenters who did not. Specifically, the audiences judged these presenters to be better prepared and more persuasive than those using no visuals.

Lawyers use exhibits; engineers use maps; retailers use catalogs; doctors use charts; computer analysts use graphics, Sunday School teachers use overhead transparencies. Whatever our profession or our presentation purpose, our results will be more dramatic with visuals.

Yes, visuals take time, they may cost money, and they can even create disasters. But the results are well worth the effort because they:

- command attention
- aid retention
- make the complex clear
- add variety and pizzazz to your delivery style
- underscore your preparation for your audience

Never decide to use visuals simply to jog your memory about your next point, to fill time, or to give you something to do with your hands.

Words are usually adequate with narratives, anecdotes, or humor when an energetic speaker can create a scene and carry the point with enthusiasm and colorful phrasing. But visuals have the required impact when presenting new data. With statistics, lists, trends, or similar information that cannot be easily grasped, analyzed, or retained, visuals provide the initial shock, interpretation, and then reference for later study and comparisons.

Visuals should be an integral part of your presentation, not an afterthought. When words become inadequate or easily forgotten, pictures remain. Visuals communicate quicker, better, and longer than words alone.

But visuals must be good. Your TV-age audience meditates on glitz in movies, magazines, and computer graphics. The world's worst visual is a transparency made of a typewriter page of words. Such a poor visual is worse than no visual at all.

The following are general guidelines for effective visuals and their use.

☞ 40. Visuals Should Not Dominate

"Don't become an usher in your own theater," warns speaker Ron Hoff. Don't let the media take over the audience's attention. The presentation is you, not the visuals. Your purpose is not to guide your audience from visual to visual. If that's your style, you may as well prepare a binder of your visuals and simply give it to the listeners for self-study.

You should dominate, visuals support. Depending on what types of visuals you use consider setting up your projectors or easels to the side of the room so that you can retain your place at "center stage."

☞ 41. Visuals Should Not Be a Laundry List

The next worst visual—second only to a full typewritten page—is a long list of single words or topics. Presenters are tempted to use such visuals because the list gives them an outline to speak from without the audience seeing any "notes." But using only words in your visuals defeats the purpose of the visual. Even written down in a clever way, words are not visual. Diagrams, art, line graphs, cartoons are. I'm not saying that you should never use a words-only visual, but always supplement it with other visuals that color in what's missing from the collection of words.

☞ 42. Avoid Clutter

If you do design "verbal" visuals to refer to a previous point in the presentation or to elaborate on or compare to other visuals, use no more than seven lines to a visual and no more than three or four words to a line.

Don't bombard your audience with statistics and numbers. Too many numbers dilute your main points. The audience wants to grasp the key concept (Our costs have risen 40 percent.); they'll pick up the specifics in a handout they can mull over later.

Also, avoid permitting your style of print to clutter. Words in all uppercase lettering are more difficult to read than both uppercase and lowercase. Use a uniform print size and style.

Remember balance and symmetry on the page. Print should not be crowded, off-center, or unevenly scrunched between columns or pictures.

Use adequate white space to help the eye differentiate between ideas and make comparisons and contrasts.

VISUAL DESIGN—DO'S AND DON'TS

NOT THIS:

jangling keys
folded arms
STIFF, jerky movements

tight fists
pointing fingers

coughing
throat clearing

What's the point?

BUT THIS:

NEGATIVE GESTURES
DETRACT FROM WORDS

jangling keys
folded arms

stiff, jerky movements
tight fists
pointing fingers
throat clearing

Informative captions

VISUAL DESIGN—DO'S AND DON'TS

NOT THIS:

Six-Year Survival Rate

SIZE	1-4	5-9	10-14	15-19
small	26%	65%	75%	77%
medium	34%	72%	75%	79%
large	26%	33%	48%	69%

Too crowded

BUT THIS:

SIX-YEAR SURVIVAL RATE

SIZE	1-4	5-9	10-14	15-19
small	26%	65%	75%	77%
medium	34%	72%	75%	79%
large	26%	33%	48%	69%

Balance and symmetry

VISUAL DESIGN—DO'S AND DON'TS

NOT THIS:

Percentage of Companies
Surviving after 6 years

SIZE OF COMPANY	No JOBS ADDED	1-4 JOBS ADDED
1-4 employees	26.0%	65%
5-499 employees	34.1%	72.4%

Uncentered

BUT THIS:

GROWTH AND SURVIVAL

Employment Growth	Two Years	Four Years
No jobs added	70.5%	37.5%
1-4 jobs added	92.0%	80.9%

Centered

VISUAL DESIGN—DO'S AND DON'TS

NOT THIS:

Group ASSIGNMENTS

PROJECT 1   Room 220   6pm

Project two Room 223   7:00pm

Project III Rm 224   8:00PM

Mixed lettering

BUT THIS:

GROUP ASSIGNMENTS

Project 1   Rm 220   6:00pm

Project 2   Rm 223   7:00pm

Project 3   Rm 224   8:00pm

Uniform lettering

☞ 43. Use Color for Highlighting

Besides word clutter, there's color clutter. To please the eye, add emphasis, and organize ideas, try adding color. But primarily use color as an accent—for bullet points, titles, underlining, art. Two colors are good; a third color can highlight; a fourth color clutters.

Bold colors such as blue, black, green, or purple are good for the main ideas. Accent with red. Avoid light iridescent colors that can't be seen easily.

Colors may also subliminally reinforce your message: red for caution, attention, or hostility; yellow for energy; green for growth; blue for tranquility; black for boldness.

☞ 44. Caption Each Visual

Imagine yourself strolling past your TV and catching a glimpse of action on the screen with the volume turned off. You should be able to tell what's happening after a moment or two. The same should be true of your visuals; they need to be complete enough to stand alone. Use either an informative caption or a title to telegraph the key point to the viewer.

☞ 45. Add the Light Touch

If you consider yourself a poor storyteller, inept with the timing or punchline of a joke, create built-in humor in your delivery through your visuals. With prior preparation, you can come up with clever ways to illustrate your points so they will "speak for themselves." (That's why I keep an ongoing file of cartoons and quotes.)

☞ 46. Limit the Number

Too much of a good thing dilutes its effectiveness. As long as you're preparing slides, twenty-five is not necessarily better than fifteen. Any technique, even glitzy slides, can get monotonous. As a rule of thumb, your presentation should average no more than one visual per minute. "Average" is a deceiving word here, however. For example, I may use three foils to present unclear sentences in a writing class, but then use no visuals at all for fifteen minutes of a style discussion. Variety is the key.

☞ 47. Select Visuals Appropriate to the Concept

Real objects or simulated models best demonstrate operating procedures or processes. Blow-up photos or line drawings best illustrate internal workings of equipment. Line graphs best show trends rather than exact numbers. Bar charts best illustrate high-low comparisons. Flowcharts best illustrate interactive processes or the passage of time. Pictures or cartoons best illustrate concepts. Always select the visual that best suits your purpose.

☞ 48. Add Variety

Even the best gets boring after the better part of an hour. If you select one medium for the major part of your presentation, consider other aids simply for a change of pace. In my presentations, I usually average five aids: transparencies, videos, flip charts, handouts, reference books. Then within each of these visual types, I vary the use of words, cartoons, diagrams, and photos.

☞ 49. Present the Visual, Then Pause

When first displaying your visual, pause to give the audience a couple of moments to take it in. If you immediately try to talk, they will miss your first few words while they preview what's in sight. Let them see, then they'll switch gears and begin to listen to you again as you elaborate and build your point.

☞ 50. Talk to the Audience, Not the Visuals

Never face your visuals as you talk, or worse yet, read them to your audience. Know your material well enough so that you can maintain eye contact while elaborating in your own words. The visual is the beginning point, not the end. Remember, visuals are for the audience, not the presenter.

☞ 51. Make Visuals Attractive

You may think this goes without saying. It doesn't. I recently attended a meeting with twenty-two representatives of a multi-billion-dollar company where they presented their ideas visually. Some used commercially prepared, glitzy foils and videos. Three used transparencies of typewritten notes. Keep in mind that these were trainers who make presentations for a living!

That is not to say that you have to spend a fortune having visuals done commercially. Commercially done visuals look great, but they may, in the case of a prospective buyer, convey the wrong impression (that you have plenty of money and don't need his business or monetary support for your cause). "Canned" visuals may also convey the idea that you have not taken the time to tailor your presentation to your audience.

Attractive and expensive are not necessarily synonymous. "Homemade" visuals can be very effective. Sources for artwork include the yellow pages of your phone book, coloring books, clip art, or the portfolio of the teenage art student down the street. Your own creations offer the opportunity to customize for a specific audience. You can also create them immediately without any outside turn-around time.

Sloppily done visuals convey no forethought and may produce a perception of shoddy work and a cheap image—of particular concern to a prospective customer.

☞ 52. Proofread Carefully

Misspellings, typos, inconsistency in headings and layout, and broken lettering are major distractions for the audience. A misspelling interrupts the listener's thought processes. Immediately, he or she will wonder: "Should I point this out? I wonder if the speaker's aware of this? Does she not recognize the error? Doesn't she care?" Errors damage an image of professionalism and leave the impression of hurried, inadequate preparation.

Always allow a cool-off period between production of your visuals and your practice time so that you can see them objectively and catch goofs. It's also a good idea to have others proofread them for inconsistencies and errors you might miss.

Never delegate all the proofreading to someone else or blame others when an error appears on the screen in front of your audience. The presenter is ultimately responsible for the quality of the visuals as much as the talk.

☞ 53. Idiot-Proof Them

Always title your visuals, number them, and put them in order. If you have some portable system for moving them from location to location, that's even better. We use flipframes (clear acetate pages that provide a protective cover, a clean-cut border, and an area for frame notes) that fit in a three-ring binder.

Make frame notes to jog your memory, but be brief. Most presenters err on the side of adding too many notes—so many that they can't read them at a glance.

Have an alternate game plan for getting your information across if some disaster happens that makes using your visuals impossible. A colleague of mine recently prepared a talk on communication in foreign cultures for a group of fifteen people. When she showed up to make the presentation she discovered that five of the fifteen students were blind.

☞ **54. Coordinate Your Delivery with the Visual**

Decide beforehand where you will stand as you use each visual. When using an overhead, will you stand to the left or the right of the screen? Will you need to pull the VCR monitor to the middle of the room during the video vignette or will everyone be able to see the screen at an angle?

Be careful that you do not plan to use a lectern for holding your notes and then discover you must move away from it to use the flipchart or an overhead.

If you plan to use visuals think hard about using a lectern at all. Standing behind a lectern, presenters look like "the authority" not to be questioned or interrupted. Lecterns discourage audience interaction and create a distance between you and the listeners, something you want to avoid at all costs. Also, the lectern hides most of the body language that would add enthusiasm to your delivery. In other words, lecterns take away much of what you intend to add with visuals.

Unless you're in a very formal setting in front of a very large audience, plan to move during your presentation. Use all of your "stage" as much as possible. As you complete one point, move to another spot to deliver the next idea. Your movement reduces your nervous energy and forces the audience to tune in as you begin your next idea or activity.

Physically moving from one AV aid to another also brings closure to an idea or activity and gives the audience time to make a transition in their thinking. Movement adds energy to your delivery and keeps the audience alert.

Don't, however, confuse pacing with movement. Pacing is a monotonous back-and-forth striding. Movement across the stage area in conjunction with a variety of ideas, visuals, and activity is a fluid reinforcement of the thinking process.

☞ 55. Rules for "Sit-Down" Presentations

In a business setting, particularly on sales calls, you may make presentations to only one person or possibly to two or three seated around a decision-maker's desk. Although there's absolutely no correlation between size of the audience and importance of the outcome, you have to take different settings into consideration. First of all, consider the group's expectations. Don't just assume that because the audience is small they do not expect a formal presentation—with visuals and the works.

Second, remember that because you are seated around a desk or table at eye level with the group, your enthusiasm, assertiveness, and authority must be conveyed at "half mast"—that is, primarily with your facial expressions and sitting posture. Don't let yourself slouch. Leaning forward in your chair shows enthusiasm and confidence about your subject. Leaning backward in your chair conveys openness to questions.

Above all, position yourself to maintain eye contact with everyone in the room. You don't want to be caught sitting between two listeners so that you have to glance from side to side to make each point as if you're playing Ping-Pong. Also, if possible, remove any physical obstacles that block vision or create "distance" between you and your audience—such as a shelf that juts out from the wall or plant leaves you must dodge to make eye contact. If the logistics don't look conducive to the business at hand, simply say so and make the necessary adjustments: "Do you mind if I move over to this side of the room so that these shelves don't block our view?"

After you give thought to where and how to seat yourself to address your small group, be sure to position visuals so that your audience can readily see them. Your listeners, not you, need to read them. An upside-down glance at your visual should be all you need to cue you to your next point.

A desktop-size flip chart, a portfolio, a binder, or other scaled-down "easel" will hold your visuals at close range. Of course, there's nothing wrong—and everything right—with using your regular flip chart or overhead transparencies if the necessary equipment is available. Simply keep in mind that when you're summoned on the spur of the moment to the boss' office to "give a quick update on the XYZ project," you may not have enough advance notice to locate a projector and screen. A quick change of plans about the kinds of visuals to use—a transparency turned into a handout—may be in order.

Whichever visual you select—desktop-size flipcharts, binder pages, or handouts—position them as if the desktop is your "stage," taking into consideration all the other tips mentioned in this chapter. When you hold handouts toward your audience, position the visual with the makeshift easel "gutter" at the top and use a pen or pencil as your pointer. Put visuals out of sight when you finish discussing them.

☞ **56. Practice Your Delivery Using the Aids**

Few visual aids require no practice for smooth manipulation. Running through the process in your mind is not the same as actually staging (walking through) the delivery. Try to practice in the room where you will give the presentation and get the feel of the place. Study the appropriate angles that will allow you to see notes and also to be out of the way of your audience's view.

In practicing with visuals such as slides or videos, where the equipment is located away from the "stage" area, you may discover that you need an assistant. Making that discovery beforehand prevents disasters.

☞ 57. Make Your Audience Move

I often use a variety of visuals—two flip charts, two over-head projectors and screens, a VCR for video, wall charts, and handouts. With that much equipment, appropriate delivery requires coordination. The VCR, for example, may be located at the back of the room at some client sites.

But a "scattered" stage area is no cause for concern. Your audience will move with you as you move around the room, sliding their chairs or shifting body positions to gain a better view. This movement, however slight, makes them more alert and reduces the tension of sitting in one spot and facing one direction for long periods of time.

Movement on the part of the audience is beneficial, not detrimental, to your presentation.

☞ 58. Handle Visuals Correctly

You'll need to select appropriate visuals based on the culture and expectations of the audience you'll be ad-dressing, costs of the visuals, availability of equipment, production time, size of the room and audience, seating arrangement, and lighting conditions.

The following lists present the pros and cons of each medium and tips on handling each visual effectively.

▶ **Flip Charts**
Pros:
- Easy to move around the room and close to your audience
- Inexpensive
- Easy to create
- Informal, fresh, and spontaneous
- Readily available at most sites
- Easily modified or customized on the spot

• Easily updated from presentation to presentation

Cons:
• Difficult for large audiences to see
• Time-consuming to prepare with fancy lettering and art
• Cumbersome to transport, easily worn with use
• Lacking in pizzazz—delivery style has to carry the message

Tips on using:
• Write, then talk; or talk, then write. Doing both simultaneously causes you to misspell, transpose syllables, or omit words.
• Jot any notes in pencil in the left-hand margin. They'll be visible to you but not to the audience.
• Leave one or two blank pages between each visual so the words don't show through before you're ready to reveal a page.
• Make yourself a "handle" on each page by folding up the corner of the page you want to refer to frequently or by labeling and attaching a piece of masking tape to the edge. With one motion, you can catch the tape and flip the page without fumbling.
• Position yourself to the side of the page as you write so that you will not completely lose eye contact with your audience.
• Remove pages and tape them to the walls if you need additional ones to finish a concept.
• Cover a page or at least walk away from it when you're finished.
• Use two charts simultaneously for variety—one for presenting key points, the other for elaborating with supporting detail.

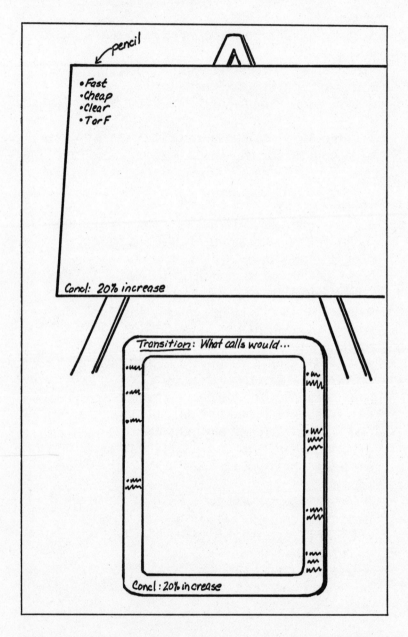

Figure 4: Jot only key words and phrases as notes in the margins of flip charts or on overhead frames.

◗ Overhead Transparencies

Pros:

- Suitable for small or large audiences up to 400 people
- Easy and quick to create
- Transportable
- Well-thought-out and professional appearance
- Easy to control and display only parts of the lines with a cover page
- Easily updated and maintained
- Versatile with color, overlays, drawings, reproductions of photos or diagrams from magazines, newspapers, books and so forth

Cons:

- Awkward manipulation without practice

Tips for using:

- Use bullets with key words and phrases only, not complete sentences.
- Expose only a line at a time if you intend to elaborate point by point.
- Jot brief notes on the frame.
- Frame them in cardboard or flipframes for ease of handling.
- Turn the projector light off or cover the light with a piece of cardboard before you position the first one and while you switch transparencies.
- Place a blank transparency over a printed one so that you can add highlighting or extra words without altering the original.
- Leave room lights up.
- Stand next to the screen rather than the projector when possible to prevent blocking the audience's view.
- Use large sweeping gestures when you point to the screen.
- Use a pointer when pointing to the projector base.

- Avoid packing up and filing your transparencies during your closing comments. Wait until you're completely finished with your presentation to put them away.
- Keep the original copies to make new ones when they become discolored or smudged.

▶ Slides

Pros:
- Suitable for large audiences up to 1,000
- Highly professional appearance, indicating forethought
- Appealing range of colors and types of art
- Easy to use with a push of a button
- Transportable

Cons:
- Necessary for lights to be dimmed
- Fixed order of slides once they are placed in the carousel
- All-or-nothing view—impossible to reveal only part of a visual at a time or to highlight with an accent color as you talk
- Expensive to produce
- Difficult and expensive to update
- Formal approach—inhibits discussion and participation
- Sometimes necessary to coordinate with projectionist in sound room
- Attention focused on the visual rather than presenter

Tips on using:
- Place the screen off center so that you can stand in "center stage" position.
- Check the slide carousel before you speak for missing, extra, or upside-down slides that reflect poor preparation.
- Have paper copies of slides on your notes in front of

you so you know what comes next.
- Practice with the remote control ahead of time.
- Mount slides all in the same kind of frames to prevent hanging.

▶ Videos/filmstrips
Pros:
- Suitable for large audiences up to 1,000
- Highly professional appearance, indicating forethought
- Appealing range of colors and types of art
- Easy to use with a push of a button
- Transportable

Cons:
- Expensive to produce
- Difficult and expensive to update
- Formal approach—inhibits discussion and participation
- Attention focused on the visual rather than the presenter

Tips on using:
- Place the screen or monitor off center so that you can stand in "center stage" position.
- Set the tape counter so that you can easily cue up vignettes and fast forward or reverse to a particular segment.
- Give the audience a preview of what they will see and ask them to watch for certain things that you will refer to in later discussion.

▶ Handouts
Pros:
- Timing on the presentation unaltered because of length of handouts
- Easily maintained and updated

- Inexpensive to produce
- Interactive design—encourages audience participation
- Note taking made easy
- Enhanced recall because the audience takes away reference material

Cons:
- Difficult to transport large numbers of lengthy handouts without mailing them to the site ahead of time
- Greater danger of unauthorized copying and use of your material

Tips on using:
- Try to be as creative in your handout as with any other visual, avoiding "plain vanilla" typed pages.
- Use brightly colored paper for pizzazz.
- Tell the audience up front what's in the handouts so they'll know whether to take notes during your presentation.
- Hold them so the pages face the audience as you refer to specific points.
- Build interest in the handouts by letting the audience know that they contain information other than exactly what you've already presented orally.
- Refer to material for later reflection, for personal evaluation, or for on-the-job use.
- Distribute them *during* the presentation if they are designed to be interactive, with the audience referring to them as you ask them to list, mark, note, fill in the blanks, or otherwise react.
- Distribute them *after* your presentation if they are simply reference material for later use. Never let the audience "read along" with you because they read much faster than you talk and because you lose eye contact and control.
- Include any or all of the following: summary of your

key points, complex illustrations of key points, documentation and support from reference sources, bibliography to encourage futher reading and to give credit on ideas borrowed from others, articles for further reading, and personal data on the presenter.

◆ Objects for Demonstrations
Pros:
- Realistic reinforcement to your words
- Increased audience participation with close observation

Cons:
- Often difficult to transport
- Often expensive to replace when worn
- Often too small for audience to see the most significant parts
- Almost always difficult for large audiences to see

Tips on using:
- Use both the object and a blow-up diagram of the object for complete flexibility in referring to inside or small parts.
- Avoid passing the object around the audience while you are talking.
- Practice thoroughly any assembly or disassembly required.

Unless you have the authority of the president of the United States, the delivery style of an actor, a message of world importance, and intentions of being as brief as a commercial, design visuals into your presentation. They clarify ideas, aid retention, and create pizzazz difficult to generate in any other way.

Handling Question-and-Answer Periods

6

Next to the invitation itself, the offhanded comment, "Oh, by the way, you should allow a little time at the end for questions," is the greatest cause for concern for most presenters. Why? There are several reasons: They lack confidence in their understanding of the subject or project in general. They fear not knowing the answer to a specific question. They fear that someone will question their authority or the credibility of their information. They fear stammering and faltering with unplanned answers. They fear a hostile audience or participant. They fear losing control of the audience and the situation. They may even feel "put upon" for being placed on the spot with an unpopular answer. And any or all of these may cause embarrassment.

Why, then, should presenters put themselves through the anxiety of anticipating these predicaments and devastating results? First of all, the audience expects time for questions—as their God-given right to force the presenter to "meet the press," particularly on controversial points.

But in addition to audience expectations and needs, questions also benefit you, the presenter. First, questions allow you to apply the key points specifically to your audience's situation. Audience analysis, of course, is part of your preparation, but questions give you one last opportunity to make specific application. Questions also provide feedback on how clear you were and offer a chance to correct wrong impressions. When you get an off-the-wall question, you immediately recognize that one of your key points has been perhaps misleading for your listener.

Another advantage of question/answer periods is to establish further rapport with your audience. Your answers show that you care about individual needs and understanding. They show genuine goodwill in giving value to your audience. The question/answer period allows you to be less formal and more interactive than possibly you've been in the formal presentation. Here's your opportunity to be spontaneous and witty. And nothing shows your depth of knowledge, credibility, and communication skills as vividly as unrehearsed fielding of unplanned questions.

Finally, questioning periods give you "leeway" in judging the appropriate timing. Five or ten minutes either added or subtracted from your presentation can be corrected in the time allotted for questions—a reassuring cushion for you, particularly on first-time presentations.

Let's get into the mechanics, then, of handling question-answer periods effectively.

☞ 59. Anticipate and Prepare for Questions

Audience analysis, the first step in preparing a presentation, should always include consideration of questions the group will have about your information and opposing viewpoints. Plan for these questions specifically in your question-and-answer period and prepare a succinct response.

Here's an acronym, SEER, we use to coach students in formulating a strong, memorable, spur-of-the-moment answer:

S = Summary   (One-sentence statement of your answer)

E = Evidence   (Key points to support your answer)

E = Example   (Specific illustration that will make the key points memorable)

R = Restatement   (Restatement of summary)

For example, let's say an Exxon official is asked by an audience member about the company's handling of the widely publicized *Exxon Valdez* oil spill.

Question: "As the largest corporation in the U.S., do you really think Exxon has done all it can to clean up the oil spill in Alaska?"

Answer:

(S) "Yes, I think Exxon has done all it can to clean up the environment in the face of this disaster.

(E) "We have spent $X on transporting special equipment to the area to perform such-and-such tasks. . . . We have opened an office there and sent X people to assist in the clean-up. . . . Local government officials have asked us to do such-and-such tasks, which we have gladly done.

(E) "We even hired a special consultant to give two of our employees three weeks of training to help them perform a two-day job of nursing several sea otters back to health. We've cared about both the big things and the little things.

(R) "So, yes, I think Exxon has done all that's reasonably possible to restore the environment in the face of these tragic circumstances."

Question: "Do you think leasing space in this building will solve our overcrowding problem permanently?"

Answer:

(S) "No, I can't see leasing more space here as a permanent solution.

(E) "The extra space available is not suitable for the kinds of shelving we want to install. For another thing, the extra space does not open to the outside corridor, and therefore, the traffic to the welcome desk will still create waiting lines. And neither will the extra leasing space accommodate the additional 200 or so visitors we plan to have during the spring.

(E) "If you'll remember, two years ago we tried—with no success—to alter the traffic pattern by leasing more space in our outlying buildings. People just would not walk to the end of the hall to take the alternate route. You remember Frank Tanner's comments about people not even having time to *reach* the coffee machine in fifteen minutes, much less get a cup of coffee.

(R) "So, no, I don't consider leasing more space in this building as a permanent solution to the overcrowding problem."

With this format, you should find it much easier to be a SEER and to think on your feet. The idea is to have a thinking format to gather and present your ideas in a concise way for maximum impact and recall.

One last tip: You may want to avoid a particular issue in your prepared remarks on the lucky chance that the matter won't surface in the question-and-answer period. But don't count on it. Be prepared with an answer or at least an acknowledgment of any opposing viewpoint.

☞ **60. Explain How and When You Will Take Questions**

How long will you allow for questions? Will the questioners have to come to the microphone, or can they be heard from their seats? Will you ask them to voice their questions or submit them on paper? Do you want to be interrupted during your prepared comments, or would you prefer they hold questions until the end?

Generally, it's best to announce that you will call for questions at the end of your presentation. Questions in the middle of your planned presentation may interrupt your train of thought so that you find it difficult to get back on track. Interrupting questions may also interfere with the audience digesting the point you are making at that juncture. Finally, with interrupting questions, you will have to be creative in making a smooth transition from the answer back to your prepared comments. With, "Now, where was I?" as you return to your presentation outline, your questioner may feel the question was unwelcome and consequently feel embarrassed or hostile toward you.

On other occasions, you may decide to allow questions in the middle of your prepared comments—especially if they come from a boss, key decision maker, or other VIP in the group to whom you would not want to refuse an immediate answer. Sometimes, too, the presentation is so technical that questions delayed may be questions forgotten or unexplainable at a later point.

Either procedure—during or after the presentation—will work, provided you have given forethought to your methods.

☞ **61.** **Encourage Audience Questions**

Don't assume that if the group voices no questions there are none. Audience members hold their tongues for any number of reasons: They haven't shifted gears yet to active participation. They think that a question is stupid and that they should have understood your information the first time around. They may also think their question and your answer would be of limited interest and, therefore, hate to monopolize others' time for their own clarification. They may feel particularly inept at wording their question. They may not want to risk others' hostility with a controversial viewpoint or question.

Here are your three greatest worries: They may not have understood your presentation well enough to ask a question. They may have no interest at all in your subject. Or they may have written you off for credibility reasons.

To encourage questions, make sure your body language shows openness to the audience—upturned palms, wide-open arms, alert posture, raised eyebrows, a smile, movement toward the audience. All these gestures and movements show that you welcome their interaction.

Extend an invitation to questions with comments such as: "What questions do you have?" rather than "Do you have questions?" The least effective invitation is to mumble, "Are there questions?" as you glance up briefly and then leaf through your notes again. "Fine. If there are no questions, I'll move along so we can finish on time."

Affirmations from you after questions ("Excellent question," "Thank you for asking that," "I'm glad someone brought that up because. . . .") also encourage other listeners to take a risk with their own questions.

If you anticipate difficulty in generating questions, you can distribute index cards at the beginning or end of the session, asking participants to jot their questions down and pass them to the front. That way, you can weed through the cards, selecting the best ones. This procedure gives you maximum control and flexibility while still being responsive to the audience.

You can also generate questions with an opinion poll: "How many of you think that it would be feasible to raise this amount of money in six months' time? In a year?" They raise their hands after each. "Lisa, you responded on six months. What gives you that confidence?" Such probing relaxes the group, encourages openness, and starts momentum for expressing opinions.

Pose your own question: "A question many groups frequently ask and one that may also be of interest to you is. . . . " Or, "A question Bill Maxwell raised at our last meeting may still warrant discussion. He wanted to know if. . . ." Or, "An issue I didn't get into in my earlier remarks is Z—do any of you have a particular concern about how . . . ?"

Or you may want to repeat questions or comments overheard at a break or at the beginning: "I overheard someone before the session express the idea that. . . . How many of you agree?" This help on your part gives audiences time to consider their own questions and shows that you're taking their questions seriously.

Maybe most important of all: When you do receive a question, be brief in your answer. If you take ten minutes to answer the first one or two, some participants will fear antagonizing less interested audience members by asking another question that may lengthen your presentation another half hour.

☞ 62. To Repeat or Not Repeat, That Is the Question

If the sound is so poor in the room that questions from the audience can't be heard, certainly you should repeat them for all to hear. You may want to repeat some questions, if not all, simply to give yourself time to think.

But to repeat a question in a small-group setting where everyone obviously heard is redundant and makes you sound like a parrot.

And you never want to repeat hostile questions because it's difficult to do so without sounding hostile or defensive yourself. The other danger is that you reinforce the negative thought or the opposing viewpoint in your audience's mind.

☞ 63. Maintain Control of the Audience

Set boundaries at the beginning of the session as to what kinds of questions you will take, the number of questions you have time for, and who will respond to each.

"I'll ask you not to bring up the issues of X and Y for security reasons." "We won't let ourselves get into the Z matter because of the current litigation." "I prefer to deal with questions only in the area of A and B rather than C, which headquarters can more appropriately deal with." All these comments at the beginning set the stage for your control of what is to follow.

Then when someone asks an irrelevant question, you can defer the answer to a private dialogue at the break and not waste the group's time or seem unresponsive to their needs. You will also limit the occasion for questions unrelated to your expertise or experience.

And no one says that you must answer all the questions. If you consider a question out-of-line, confidential, personal, irrelevant, or of little interest to the rest of the group, you can always deflect it, reroute it, challenge it, or simply defer answering it. "I'm afraid that's out of my area of expertise; would someone else like to respond?" "Jack, I'm curious about why you're asking that question; didn't you and Mark work those issues out earlier?" "Do we really need to answer that question, or would it be more advantageous to focus on . . . ?"

Finally, take questions in turn and don't let a few monopolize: "Henry, can you hold off a moment. I think I saw Jack's hand first." Or, "I regret that we'll not have time to finish with all the questions from those of you who are so perceptive with additional thoughts. But we do need to wrap this up. I'll be around here for a few minutes and back in my office all afternoon if any of you would like to follow up one on one."

☞ 64. Listen to the Question

Listening to the questions may not be as easy as it sounds. If you're nervous, if you're lambasting yourself about a previous error, if you're worrying about the time, or if you're threatened by the hostile body language of someone in the room, it's easy to miss the point of what the questioner is asking. Poor listening may cause you to fumble a question you could have easily fielded.

Compounding the matter is the fact that the questioner may give too much background or irrelevant information before getting to the real point. And she may not have a clear understanding of what her real question is!

To avoid giving an off-base answer, clarify with a probing question of your own: "Let me see if I understand your question correctly. You want to know if . . . ?" Or, "Is your question thus-and-so?" Or, "Are you really asking if it is possible to . . . ?"

Give your best effort to understanding the true question rather than concentrating on preparing your reply to contradict or refute the asker's viewpoint. Finally, show that you are listening with attentive body language, such as leaning forward, head tilted in reflection, and steady eye contact.

☞ 65. Think Before You Answer

Even when an answer pops quickly to mind, pause before rushing ahead. With frequently asked questions, it's tempting to give the canned answer when, with a little forethought, you can customize your answer, making it even more responsive to the asker.

To allow even more thinking time, you can use props such as removing or replacing eye glasses, taking a sip of water, striding to another spot in the room before turning to face the group, or tilting your head and rubbing your chin as if reflecting on the brilliance of the question.

You can also buy thinking time by commenting on the question itself: "That's a tough question." "That's a perceptive question." "I anticipated someone asking that and I don't know if I'm going to have an answer that you'll agree with or find completely satisfying, but. . . . "

You may say honestly: "Let me think about that a moment" and then repeat the question to yourself aloud, "Ummm, what would I recommend if . . . " Such a pause renews the audience's attention as they anticipate why the question required serious reflection.

You may refuse to answer at all: "I'm not at liberty to answer that now." "That piece of the puzzle is still in the works now. May I get back to you on that later?"

☞ **66.** Overview Your Answer Briefly, Then Elaborate

The question-answer period is not the place to redo your presentation points. When asked a question, respond with a headline message, then elaborate very briefly. Your audience will understand the elaboration much better within the context of your overview answer.

Here are a couple of examples of this technique: "In a word, my answer is yes. Management is aware of the problem and we're trying to correct it. Last week, for example. . . . " Another example of overviewing and then elaborating: "I don't think it's too expensive, no. It costs less than X and Y. Here's how I think we can finance the first phase. . . . "

☞ **67.** Direct Answers to the Entire Audience

Begin your answer while maintaining eye contact with the asker, and then after a few seconds glance away and sweep the entire group. Direct the remainder of your answer to everyone and make your comments generic enough for their interests also.

Remember that you do not have to satisfy every questioner completely because some will never stop their follow-up questions. Others may persist in presenting their own viewpoints even after you've given your answer. Keep in mind that you don't have to answer every question fully. Just make your point briefly, break eye contact with the asker, and turn to the entire group, looking for the next question.

☞ 68. Answering to Reinforce Your Points

"I'm glad you brought that issue up because it will give me opportunity to elaborate on . . . " realigns the question with one you really want or need to answer. You can also refocus the question to make it bigger or smaller: "The larger issue that most of the industry will be concerned with is . . . ; therefore, let me put my answer in a larger context." Or, "Yes, that is the big-picture problem, but let me bring it a little closer to home with the more direct issue of. . . . "

Go in either direction with the question to reinforce what you think is the essential message of interest.

☞ 69. Handling "Problem" Questions

Inevitably, every public speaker will at times face difficult questions from his or her audience. The following descriptions of such typical questions will give you an opportunity to polish your techniques for handling them.

▶ Show-off Questions
These are the questions asked merely to show the asker's own knowledge of the subject or accomplishments. Recognize the reason behind the question, then comment only briefly and go to the next question. If this kind of questioner persists, you may have to add a comment such as the following to keep him or her from monopolizing the situation: "I'm not sure I'm understanding your question in all this. Would you please ask the specific question again."

The asker will generally fumble into focusing on a question that you can answer briefly and use to regain control.

◗ Off-the-Subject Questions

If the question is completely off the wall, you may simply gaze at the asker momentarily and then move on without a response at all—as if you didn't quite understand the point. Then ask if someone else has a similar concern. If so, answer briefly. If not, ask for permission to hold the question until the end, "if there's time."

Or you may comment: "Interesting idea, but how does that relate to Y?" The asker will usually mumble that it doesn't and acquiesce or ask a more relevant question.

"That's interesting and something worth further thought, but right now I'd like to spend our time focusing on..." will usually put the matter to rest. Or, "I hadn't expected a question of that nature in this session. May we discuss that later—just you and I?" The asker will usually be reinforced by the personal attention offered and you won't lose the rest of the audience.

◗ Limited-Interest Questions

When possible, bridge from the limited perspective to the larger issue at hand: "With reference to your specific situation, my opinion is that..., but the larger issue here seems to be...." Continue by making application to the entire audience.

Ask, "Does anyone else here have that concern?" Pause and look around, then continue: "Well, let me give you a brief answer and let's talk about that later one on one—will that be more helpful?"

Then break eye contact and move on.

◗ "Dumb" Questions

Don't chance cutting off someone who asks what *sounds* like a "dumb" question but may be a very intelligent one after all. Rather, the "dumb" question may be a result of advanced, complex thinking that may not have occurred to you. The question may be quite relevant and you simply don't understand the relevance because of limited

146 The Confident Communicator

expertise. Probe further to make sure you understand completely: "I'm afraid I'm not following the question. Would you explain further exactly how X relates to Y?"

◗ Rambling or Long-winded Questions
You may interrupt with, "Excuse me, but do I understand your central question to be . . . ?" Or, "Excuse me, but I think I now have the drift of your question. My response is simply that . . . "

◗ Unintelligible Questions
If you cannot understand the question because the asker has a heavy dialect or is fuzzy in his wording, pick one phrase or part of the question to deal with and frame a question that you think he or she may be asking.

◗ Multiple Questions
In response to long, complex questions with irrelevant information thrown into the pot, you may have difficulty remembering everything that was asked along the way. When that's the case, either answer the questions you remember, answer the last one, answer the most important one, or ask the questioner to repeat them slowly while you write them down. Then respond one by one.

You can defer some of them with: "If I understand completely, you've asked me four good questions. Let me answer the first two and come back to the others later if there's time."

◗ Hypothetical Questions
Be careful that you don't get trapped here. Express your disagreement with assumptions and say so when you think such a situation is highly unlikely. End with, "I prefer to concern myself with the real here-and-now in formulating policy on this issue. For the present situation, I still consider. . . . "

Or refocus with, "James, we have so many real-life

situations at hand that I'd rather stick with those concrete facts, if you don't mind." Or, "There are so many unknowns and variables in hypothetical questions that it would be difficult to give a meaningful answer to that concern. In the case of Z, is your interest more about . . . ?"

◗ "Yes or No" Questions

If you can answer with a simple yes or no, do so. But if you prefer not to see the matter in black or white, say so: "I think we have to be careful here not to back ourselves into a corner with either answer. Either simple answer can keep us from seeing the extenuating circumstances that might alter. . . . " Or, "I don't think a simple yes or no would do justice to the issue." Or, "I think we'd make a mistake to put it in either/or terms. There are so many issues that can affect. . . . "

Finally, you can expand your options: "I think we have more than those two alternatives. Rather than A or B, a third possibility is to. . . . "

◗ Questions You Don't Know the Answer to

You may defer the question to someone in the room with more expertise in that area: "I'm not sure I can adequately elaborate on that. Susan, will you offer your expertise here?" You will win respect for your honesty and the support of the more experienced person you deferred the question to.

Never be afraid to say simply, "I don't know. I'll have to check on that information and get back to you." And then do so. Once a chemist at Mobil Oil asked me a question that I'd never considered in my ten years of speaking on the subject. I gave her an "I think" answer, admitted that I couldn't say for sure, and promised to locate the answer and get back to her. Back in my office in Houston the next day, I called her long-distance with the answer. She was flabbergasted that I'd followed through. Did my lack of an answer damage credibility? Not as far as I can tell—word of my "thoroughness" rapidly spread through her division.

◗ Hostile Questions

If you expect hostile questions, you may request that all questioners state their names, companies, and titles before they ask questions. Some will think twice before they blurt out a hostile comment and risk associating it with their company. Anonymity is great protection.

Try to determine the reason for any hostility. By acknowledging and sympathizing with the legitimate feelings of the asker, you may defuse the hostility and help him or her receive your answer in a much less hostile manner.

The questioner's hostility may be a reflection of his business agenda or his personality and may have little to do with you. Simply let the asker vent his emotions, and then go to the next question after a brief statement of your opinion.

Some questioners use a pseudo-courteous tone to wrap a hostile question. If so, reply just as courteously, but without the sarcasm.

You may even try a little humor or drama before answering, such as throwing your hand across your heart as if you'd been shot. "You may have hit me on that one." Then proceed to answer as calmly as you can.

For frivolously hostile questions, you can relay the question back to the asker or to another person: "Sharon, do you want to try to answer his question?" "Mark, I feel uncomfortable in responding to that question. Maybe you'd just like to tell us how you would answer that question were you in my place?"

If you think the hostility is limited to one person's viewpoint, you can let the group respond on your behalf: "Do any of the rest of you agree with that viewpoint? Does anyone else want to respond?" The silence will be a great answer. Or you may add your own in a courteous way.

Don't feel that you have to refute the opposing view in great detail, particularly if the hostile view was not well supported itself. Simply comment: "No, I don't think that's the case." No elaboration. Your answer will sound authoritative and final and will put the asker in the position of being rude and argumentative if he/she rephrases and continues.

If you can easily do so, rephrase a legitimate question minus the hostile tone: The question is: "Why are you *demanding* six years of experience for any subcontracting work?" Repeat the question aloud: "Why do we think six years' experience is necessary? Well, first of all. . . . "

Above all, do not match hostility with hostility; instead, try to remain congenial in your answer. The audience will almost always side with (or at least empathize with and respect) the person who remains the calmest and most courteous.

"A soft answer turns away wrath" (Prov. 15:1). Remember that the way you answer questions will always be remembered more clearly and for much longer than the content of your answer.

☞ 70. Conclude the Q & A Period with a Summary

Don't let your presentation limp to a close after the last question with "Well, if there are no more questions, that's about all, folks." Instead, firmly conclude with a recap of your main points and the key message. Here is where you actually use your prepared closing—that pithy quote or challenging question that will leave your audience charged and ready to act. In fact, some presenters prepare two closings: the one that ends their prepared talk and leads into the question-answer period and then one that wraps up the entire presentation time with high impact.

If you're lucky, you may happen to get a question that's

a great lead-in to your prepared closing. If so, use it as impetus to your conclusion and you'll look even more eloquent and in control.

Maybe the very idea of questioning got off to a bad start when we as children were told never to question our parents' decisions or commands. And schools sometimes reinforce the idea that questions negatively challenge the instructor's authority. Certainly, we all remember the loudmouthed smart aleck whose every question was a challenge. Or maybe we've seen too many TV dramas where the judge instructs the witness in a booming tone: "Just answer the question."

Don't let those experiences keep you from making your presentation all it can be. Allow questions and watch your audience's mood, interest, and body language switch from low gear to high. Questions clarify, tailor, and reinforce your key points. To your audience, they are your statement of openness, genuineness, courtesy, and goodwill.

Controlling the Environment

7

If it can go wrong, it will. That's why giving a good presentation starts long before the attendees arrive. You as the presenter cannot depend on anybody but yourself to check out the room, the equipment, and the entire atmosphere in time to prevent problems.

In New York's Jacob Javits Convention Center I was giving a presentation in which my visuals played a key part. Twenty minutes into the session, there was a power failure and we plunged into total blackness for half an hour.

On another occasion, I arrived at the assigned room in the Dallas Convention Center to find that we had more people than space and chairs. Half of my audience had to endure an entire ninety-minute session while seated on the floor in the aisles, in the back of the room, behind display tables, at my feet, and underneath and behind the projector screen.

At one client's office I arrived an hour early to begin my room set-up only to find that there was another meeting going on in the same conference room—scheduled to conclude at the exact moment mine was to begin. I had exactly sixty seconds to let that group exit, unpack my catalog case, find and set up the projector and screen, locate and move the VCR from the third floor, and distribute handouts and name cards.

At another client's session, I arrived an hour early to set up the room only to find another early arrival—one who was quite angry at his boss for having given him the incorrect starting time. He had scrawled an obscenity on the porcelain board in the back of the room and badgered me to guess its meaning.

And some goofs were of my own making. Speaking to a gathering of straitlaced financial people—a CEO of an international banking system, the president, and twelve executive vice presidents—I spilled a Coke someone had placed on the table holding my materials. Ten minutes into the presentation, with one spontaneous sweeping hand gesture, I knocked the Coke to the floor, splashing myself and all my materials in its path. Frozen, I stood watching it puddle into the plush carpet of their executive meeting room.

Some goofs even turn out to be funny—at least to the audience. At IBM in front of a gathering of gregarious sales reps, I was making the point that the style in business writing is much less formal now than in past decades. "For example," I elaborated, "when you're introduced to someone, you rarely respond, 'How do you do.' Instead, you say something like, 'Hello,' or 'Nice to meet you.'"

Carried away by the lucidity of my analogy, I continued, "And when was the last time your family all dressed formally and sat down to the dinner table together? I know our family doesn't dress for dinner."

A sales rep in the audience raised his hand, "May we come?" The audience roared with laughter, leaving me dumbfounded. Somebody in the front row had to point out to me what I'd actually said versus what I'd meant.

I could go on. The things that can go wrong are endless:

- The cord of the AV equipment won't reach the outlet.
- The extension cord has a three-pronged plug, and the outlet is for two prongs.
- The projector on/off switch has a short.
- The flipchart stand is too high to reach.
- The flipchart pad has only two pages left.
- The screen is lopsided so that all your visuals look as though somebody wrote them lying down.
- There's no table to put your materials on.
- Carpenters are next door tearing out the center wall.
- Hecklers are marching in the hallway, harassing your attendees.
- The restrooms can't be reached in less time than a brisk twenty-minute walk.
- The room seats 500 and you're expecting 15.
- The room seats 15 and you're expecting 500.
- The carpet smells like insecticide and the lady in the front row is wheezing and threatening a lawsuit.
- The lighting flickers, causing migraines for the people seated in the center of the room.

Oh, yes, in the situations I mentioned earlier, I had checked with the meeting planner to see that the conference room was going to be empty, that the hotel had extra projectors, and that there was sufficient seating for the audience.

But sometimes, things seem to get lost in translation. On other occasions, the meeting planner gives you all kinds of assurances simply to keep you from worrying and to get you off her phone.

Just remember that if your audience is uncomfortable, if the visuals can't be seen, if the projector has a short, if the air stinks, you are ultimately the one responsible. It's in poor taste to blame the meeting planner, the sponsor, or anyone else. You are the one the audience will blame for not taking care of the details.

The answer to such dilemmas lies in thorough planning beforehand. Why the effort? Environment can either enhance or detract from the impact of the message.

Likewise, you should have a checklist for room accommodations and equipment, and verify each and every item on your list.

71. Room and Equipment Checklist

Contact person in charge of problems: _____

Room:
Arrangement—classroom style, rows, tables, U-shaped?
Size and seating capacity?
Location of speaker table?
Podium or raised dais?
Lighting and controls?
Window lighting and controls?
Window distractions?
Wall decor interfering with visuals or activities?
Temperature controls?
Pencil sharpeners?
Clock?
Location of outlets?
Two-pronged or three-pronged outlets?
Water glasses and pitchers?
Seats facing so that vision is unblocked?

Facilities:
Signs for arriving attendees?
Parking arrangements?
Charges?
Security requirements?
Entrances unlocked?
Restroom locations?
Water fountains?
Vending machines?
Snack areas?
Coatracks?
Smoking areas?
Copy machine?
Fax machine?
Phones for internal use? External calls?
Stairs or elevator locations?
Fire alarms/procedures/ drills planned?

Equipment:
Microphone:
Lavaliere attachment working?
Extension cord for movement?
Sound level?
Back up?
Taping to be done?
Any clicking sounds such as jewelry hitting against the mike?
Flip chart:
Correct height?
Enough paper?
Markers? Dried up? Right colors?

Boards:
Correct height?
Clean surface?
Markers? Dried up? Right colors? Erasable or permanent?
Erasers?
Cleaning solution?

Overhead Projector:
  Spare bulbs?
  Focus knobs working?
  Extension cord?
  Clean surface?
  Pointer nearby?
  Space for transparencies
    nearby?

Slide Projector:
  Spare bulb?
  Focus knobs working?
  Tray cued to first slide?
  Order of slides?
  Remote control working?
  Projectionist to operate
    it?

Movie Projector:
  New bulb?
  Focused to fill screen?
  Sound working?
  Threading of film?
  Film cued to title frame?
  Remote control working?
  Projectionist to operate
    it?

VCR:
  Size of cassette tape?
  Cued to appropriate
    place?
  Reset button working?
  Appropriate TV channel
    for access?
  Volume level?
  Remote control working?

Outside interference?
Screens:
  Legs stable and sturdy?
  Located to project
    visuals at the appro-
    priate size?
  Color of background easy
    to reflect?
  Pointer nearby?
  Visible to all attendees?

Supplies:
  Note pads?
  Pencils and pens or felt-
    tip markers?
  Blank transparencies?
  Name cards? (Size to be
    read from a distance?)
  Badges?
  Attendance sheets?
  Agenda or outline of
    session?
  Handouts, order blanks?
  Reference library?
  Demo objects?
  Tape for paper?
  Push pins or tacks?
  Tape for taping electrical
    cords to the floor?
  Rubber bands?
  Paper clips?
  Index cards?
  Clock for speaker?
  Visuals for speaker?
  Extension cords?

Memories of disasters and near disasters generated most of the items on this checklist. So if this list sounds like more detail than you want to concern yourself with, get help. Either take along a friend, or work closely with the meeting planner to check out every possible glitch.

☞ **72. Distractions in the Surroundings**

The preceding checklist enables you to "troubleshoot" ahead of the meeting time. However, there are yet other potential problems for which you need to be prepared— surprises that may come your way.

▶ Power Failures or Outside Noises
If you have disasters over which you have absolutely no control or no warning—such as a power failure or improperly working equipment—simply stop the presentation and locate someone who can help.

If the distraction is outside noise, call for an unscheduled break and see if you can deal with it. If not, make a joke of it and continue. Continually referring to the noise and showing irritation increases the distraction. If you ignore it, your audience will generally follow your lead.

▶ Hecklers
Generally, if hecklers create a real distraction, they will gain the hostility of the group and provoke sympathy for you. Ignore them if they are not obtrusive. If they gain the audience's attention, speak directly to them to call attention to the fact that others came to hear your views. Remember that you control the microphone.

If you are expecting a hostile audience or outside hecklers, you can always ask the attendees to give you their names and company names at the beginning of the presentation. With their anonymity gone, they are often more hesitant to express their hostility openly.

Another way to control hecklers is to physically move

closer to them—although your tendency is to do the opposite! Making direct eye contact, approaching them, and courteously asking why they are protesting your presentation will defuse some of their hostility. At the least, your sincere approach decreases the probability that they will be rude to you personally—even if they never consider changing their views.

♦ Side Conversations

Side conversations present another challenge. Members of your audience may be talking to each other for any number of reasons. Someone arrived late and is asking a neighbor what's going on. The presentation is uninteresting to them. The tired group needs a break. The talker disagrees with your point and wants others to know it.

If you can determine the reasons for the side conversations, you can handle them more appropriately. If someone needs an explanation and the conversation seems to be coming to an end momentarily, try to ignore the distraction. If the talker wants to ask a question or express an opposing view, offer that opportunity or at least acknowledge that position: "I know that some of you have experiences and ideas to the contrary, and I'll be happy to have you express those at the end of my presentation."

If the group needs a break, give one.

If the topic is uninteresting, change your game plan and seek more audience involvement. Take an opinion poll on your current point.

If two people are simply catching up on the corporate grapevine or otherwise just enjoying each other's company, walk in their direction as you speak. All eyes will follow you as you move, and the talkers will feel the others' attention focused on them. Usually this body language and positioning will stop any such conversations.

♦ Latecomers

They are late to begin with and they are late returning

from the breaks. Never stop your presentation to "catch up" the late arriver; you will lose the rest of your group. Always start on time, letting latecomers find out what they missed from others. And when you give a break, announce the start-back time and point to the wall clock. They'll remember the time better.

Additionally, try to give them something to look forward to immediately after the break. For example, a strategically planned break will allow you to take an opinion poll right before the break and announce and interpret the results immediately after the break.

On the other hand, you may decide to ride the fence about the start-on-time principle so that your key decision-maker, who's still out of the room, doesn't miss a strategic point. A good technique to "have it both ways" is to begin the session on time but to use some kind of filler (such as cartoons or a humorous story related to your point) at the beginning so that the latecomer gets into the room in time to hear your "real" opening.

▶ Out-of-Control Audience

The cause may be a freak incident. In a large meeting in a Baylor University auditorium, a young page edged through the curtains at the side of the stage and quietly made her way with a note to a speaker seated directly behind the speaker at the podium. The page gently touched the seated speaker on the shoulder—who, startled, leaped from his chair with a loud scream. The audience roared and the speaker at the podium stopped abruptly, completely puzzled about why his colleague would suddenly spring from his chair with a yelp.

Needless to say, after such incidents or power failures or whatever, you have to let the air clear before you regain control of the group. After the laughter has died down, the noise has stopped, or the problem has been corrected, begin again in one of several ways: Tell a personal experience or joke related to what has just happened. Or simply acknowledge the interruption, then begin again. If you've forgotten where you were, ask the audience. They'll show sympathy and oblige you. Recap your main points up to that interruption and continue.

◗ Working with What You Can't Change
Obviously, unless you're the President of the United States, things will from time to time be out of your control, or you won't have the time, the help, the freedom, or the inclination to change them. So let's talk about working with less-than-desirable conditions.

If the room is too large for the audience and the attendees are scattered everywhere, ask them to move closer together up front. Their proximity will make it easier for you to generate enthusiasm and maintain eye contact.

Whatever size the room is and however it is arranged, move the equipment and furniture around so that there are exit aisles. People who feel trapped during your presentation tend to grow resistant to you and the others—even hostile. Generally, a wider arrangement with only a row or two is preferable to several narrow rows. The wider, the better to stimulate discussion.

Just be sure that you arrive early enough to find the solution to potential problems and to make any necessary adjustments in your plans.

◗ Distractions Caused by You
Comedian Steve Allen relates this story on himself. He once delivered a talk while suffering from a bad cold. At one point, he was sniffing so badly that he had to stop his presentation: "Ladies and gentlemen, if you'll forgive me, I'm suffering from quite a heavy cold and—believe it or not—I'm just going to have to stop for a moment and blow my nose. If you'll excuse me?" He did and they did.

Some distractions can't be foreseen or avoided. I once dropped an entire set of 172 transparencies when the projector table lost a leg.

But some distractions could and should be avoided: misspelled words on your visuals, an out-of-focus projector, mumbling over lost notes and slides, Coke cups sitting in a dangerous place.

Whatever the distraction—preventable or otherwise—just remember that most audiences are forgiving and sympathetic. Goofs remind them that you're human, have weaknesses, get flustered, make mistakes, and experience frustrating circumstances and challenges—all of which make you seem more like them.

They will follow your lead about how to react to distractions. If you treat the incident as a major setback, the group will focus on it and become annoyed at you or the circumstance to the point of minimizing your ideas.

On the other hand, if you apologize, downplay the distraction, regain your composure, and correct the problem quickly, they will just as quickly revert their attention back to your presentation.

Distractions—both ones you can control and can't control—will happen. Do everything you can to foresee them and minimize their potential. Then relax and take the surprises in hand. Who said speaking before a group couldn't be adventuresome?

EPILOGUE

SO YOU'RE UP NOW

"Your speech changed my life. I'll never be the same person again because of you."

"Your comments were right on target—I share your values completely."

"Your talk was so moving, you had people weeping. They were enthralled."

"Powerfully persuasive. I'm ready to sign on the dotted line."

"The way you speak—I think we're going to have to get you into a more visible position in the company. How about the new title of _____, at a $15,000 increase?"

Visualize yourself receiving these comments from an appreciative audience. Such remarks will make all the preparation and pre-speaking jitters worthwhile. There are few things more satisfying in life than to know you have influenced others to your way of thinking—whether it's to buy a product or to change the course of their life.

Yes, you can do it. The silent majority has been silent too long. Now that you have a bag of tricks and techniques, speak up with confidence!

Date Du